Airmail Antics

By
Fred Boughner

Published by Amos Press, Inc., 911 Vandemark Road, Sidney, Ohio 45365. Amos Press also publishes *Linn's Stamp News*, the world's largest and most informative stamp newspaper, and the Scott line of stamp catalogs, albums and publications.

033054   ISBN 0-940403-08-0

Introduction

Although I had collected United States airmail stamps in prior years, it wasn't until sometime in the mid-1960s that my interests turned to airmail covers. The stamps had marked airmail rate changes, but the covers did something far more intriguing. Properly arranged, they were historical records of flights that sent the first 1918 airmail service from Washington, Philadelphia and New York onward to Chicago, Omaha, Cheyenne and, ultimately, San Francisco.

Behind the history was something still more fascinating: tales of people and great adventures. I began to dig into the stories of the individuals, ideas and events that made this airmail saga happen. Why would otherwise rational human beings attempt to fly fragile airplanes made of bamboo, wood and fabric into storms, snow, wind and darkness? Such people, in the early days of the 20th century, had to have been every bit as brave and adventurous as the later astronauts who ventured into space.

The 1960s timing for me was fortuitous. Early airmail pioneers, such as Reuben Fleet, Hamilton Lee and others, still lived — though many were in their 70s and 80s. I corresponded with several and talked with a few. Their comments and recollections added life to the details in history books. Most are now gone.

They created an airmail service that was to become the foundation stone for today's commercial aviation complex. The first non-military use of the airplane was to carry mail. Until the airmail, it had been used only to bomb, strafe and reconnoiter. Today's airlines — all of them — trace their origins back to Western Air Express, Varney Airlines, National Air Transport or some early airmail carrier.

A few visionary crews of pilots, mechanics and postal officials began it all. Many gave their lives for it. These are a few of their stories . . .

Fred Boughner

Contents

Chapter 1

'The Bad Stamp'

For anyone who has studied the early days of the American airmail story, there is only one sensible conclusion: that we have airmail service at all today is only slightly less than a miracle. Early in the airmail history of the United States, much of the American public was against the "nonsense" of sending letters — or anything else — by plane. Some of the opposition was based on the fact that the United States was at war during the year of the first airmail flight in 1918. Many felt that the planes and military pilots were needed to fight the Kaiser, not to carry cards and letters up among the clouds.

Congress itself had been reluctant to start air postal service at all. The United States Post Office Department had asked Congress as early as 1912 for $50,000 to begin an experimental airpost service. The Post Office was turned down. Each year thereafter — from 1912 to 1916 — the Post Office asked again, and each request was spurned. Congress thought that it was following the will of the people in these rejections.

The Post Office approved several exhibitionist barnstorming flights carrying small amounts of mail for very short distances at no expense to the Post Office. Finally, in 1916, Congress granted funds for a test. No special appropriation was made; instead, the monies were taken from the Steamboat and Power Boat Fund.

The Post Office promptly advertised for private carrier bids on postal flights in Massachusetts and Alaska. No one answered the bids. The surmise is that there was a lack of suitably constructed planes to enable private carriers to haul mail at a profit. The funds expired unused. However, World War I continued to spur the development of aircraft for military purposes, and Congress again, in 1918, appropriated $100,000 for establishment of an experimental airmail route. This time it was determined that the Post Office would operate the mail-handling and delivery portion with the Army supplying the planes, pilots and maintenance from the new Air Corps arm of the military.

Captain Benjamin Lipsner of the United States Army was appointed the first superintendent of aerial mail for the Post Office Department. He, along with Otto Praeger, second assistant postmaster general, and others had been prime movers in the push for an airmail service.

Then came what Lipsner termed "the bad stamp." The stamp to be used for the first airmail service was of very minor importance to Lipsner, Praeger and others who were not stamp collectors. But their concern greatly increased when the famous inverted-plane error appeared two days prior to the first scheduled flight. The advocates of airmail feared the stamp error would give new ammunition to their opponents, who believed the whole project was ridiculous, unnecessary and fraught with bungling.

Students of United States airmail stamps know that the first issue, the 24¢ bicolor Jenny, as well as the rest of the first airmail stamps, were not purely airmail stamps. The word "airmail" does not even appear on any of these adhesives. They all were used for other types of postage as well. This explains why the 24¢ issue went on sale May 13

— two days prior to the first airmail flight. The stamp's first usage was on regular mail, not on airpost, and that is why the "bad stamp" was found before Lipsner's first plane had even left the ground.

It was on May 14, 1918, that lucky plate block collector William T. Robey purchased a pane of 100 stamps featur-

The "bad" stamp that worried early airmail officials.

ing the inverted-center error. For a while, it was thought that three more such panes of 100 stamps each existed from this one sheet of upside-down Jenny stamps that crossed the post office counter and fell into the hands of Robey. He held out against strong official pressure to surrender the pane, since he believed he had purchased it in a proper manner.

It was later learned that this 24¢ stamp was printed in sheets of but a single 100-subject pane, and no other inverts were ever reported. Be that as it may, as Lipsner said in his book, *Jennies to Jets,* "I was afraid that the airmail service, already subject to much ridicule, would be further embarrassed."

From a philatelic standpoint, the inverted Jenny is the reason the word "TOP" appears on pane selvage of early bicolored, flat-plate-produced airmail issues. The 24¢

stamp was printed with two plates — one for the carmine rose frame and one for the blue airplane vignette. After the error, the Bureau of Engraving and Printing quickly added the word "TOP" to each color plate in an attempt to prevent further printing inversions. This practice continued through other bicolor issues, such as the 5¢ Beacon of 1928, the 16¢ combination airpost special delivery of

During the third printing of the 24¢ Jenny airmail stamp of 1918, an additional "TOP" was placed in red in the selvage to help inspectors spot any further inverts.

1936, and the 6¢ Eagle of 1938. After 1938, no bicolor airmails were printed until the 7¢ Jupiter Balloon issue of 1959. By that time, the Giori Press technique eliminated the need for the "TOP" designation.

But the embarrassment of the "bad stamp" remained, and for those dedicated men who pioneered the first flight of mail, it was, unfortunately, only the beginning. The disaster of the first airmail flight, the battles to overcome public apathy, and the pure courage of the people involved in the beginnings of an airmail service make a story of hilarious mistakes and supreme faith.

Chapter 2

The Little Giant

Throughout the early years of the airmail — roughly from 1918 to 1930 — the service was fortunate to have a quartet of capable postal administrators in the front office. None of them was an aviator; none of them ever became postmaster general. All of them held the same title of second assistant postmaster general at one time or another. This position forced all four of them to become directly involved with the airmail, since the basic responsibility of the postmaster's second assistant in those days was to guide and improve all modes of transport used to move the mails.

Even though they were not pilots, they "flew" the front office with such enthusiasm and vigor that, in retrospect, it is hard to see how the airmail could have succeeded without them. They dreamed the dreams, set the goals, manuevered the politicians, fought the red tape and secured the congressional support and monies that built the Aerial Mail Service. In a very real sense, they were airmail pioneers — just as much so as Max Miller, Jack Knight, Ham Lee, Torrey Webb and others who took more romantic and adventurous roles in the drama that was the airmail in its natal years. Their job was to fight governmental skepticism and public apathy. In many ways, it was a job just as difficult as battling bad weather and a balky Liberty engine.

A rather dishevelled looking, cigar-smoking little man was the first of that foursome. He held the second assistant's post during its most crucial time — from the beginnings of the airmail in 1918 through 1921, when the new Harding administration came into office. His name was

Otto Praeger, as second postmaster general, was one of the prime movers in the push for an airmail service in the United States.

Otto Praeger, and throughout any story of the airmail, collectors will find his name sprinkled liberally.

Otto Praeger was present at the conception and the christening of the United States airpost system. He, along with other luminaries, such as President Wilson, Franklin

Roosevelt, Albert Burleson and Captain Ben Lipsner, watched that first flight on May 15, 1918. Long before that ceremony, however, he had been deeply involved in all of the problems that had to be overcome first: planes, personnel, appropriations, schedules, maintenance details, and even the matter of stamp and rate selection for that first flight.

The late Major Reuben Fleet seemed to believe that Praeger at times was the only sensible man in the Post Office Department. "He backed me on occasions when no other postal official would," said Fleet. Praeger was known in Washington as an executive who could unravel red tape quickly, and when the occasion demanded it, he could be a superb persuader.

Otto Praeger was described as a visionary who believed that the air service would require a government subsidy to get a firm toehold. He was one of the first to realize that flying the mail was only a stepping stone toward the greater objective of flying passengers. As a good financial administrator, he saw the cost benefits to the airmail when this would finally happen. This was Walter Brown's later view, but Praeger had it long before Brown ever stepped into the national postal scene.

When the Post Office Department took over all airmail operations on August 12, 1918, it was Praeger who persuaded Army Captain Ben Lipsner to stay on as the new aerial mail superintendent. "You made it work for the Army, Ben; now I want you to run it for us," said Praeger. "Airmail is here to stay, and we've already got plans to expand the service clear across the country."

When Lipsner agreed to take the post, Praeger tried to get him a leave of absence from the military. When Secretary Newton Baker refused this request, Praeger then had to convince Lipsner that the long-range future of the airmail offered more rewards than an Army career. Lipsner finally resigned his commission and took the job.

Praeger became personally involved with the pilots who flew the mail. He had great respect for their courage and abilities, and frequently told them so. He has been termed "the first airmail enthusiast," and his adulation

Captain Benjamin Lipsner of the United States Army was appointed the first superintendent of aerial mail for the United States Post Office Department.

for his fliers was comparable to that of a football fan for his favorite quarterback.

When Jack Knight finished his long night flight through snow and blackness into Maywood Field, Chicago, on February 23, 1921, Praeger issued the following statement to the press immediately: "The all-night flight from Cheyenne, Wyoming, to Chicago, a distance of 839 miles, is the most momentous step in civil aviation. The Post Office some time ago directed that the airmail enter upon regular night operations, and the flight by a pilot never over that ground before, in the black of night, through snow flurries and fog drifts, with three landings for refueling and exchange of mails, is a demonstration of the entire feasibility of commercial night flying. It will mean the speedy revolutionizing of letter transportation methods and practices throughout the world." It is obvious that Praeger did not mind using either a few superlatives or some long sentences in his enthusiasm for Jack Knight and the airmail.

Praeger even put together some incentive plans for his pilots. In 1921 he got five newspapers to put up $1,000 prize money for the best mileage flown in a six-month period by the fliers on the transcontinental route. It was a typical Praeger move, bespeaking his very real interest in pilots as people and in their performances in the air.

Under this "little giant," the airmail took these huge strides forward: The original New York-Philadelphia-Washington route began. The mail was transferred smoothly from the Army to the Post Office Department. The Cleveland-Chicago, New York-Cleveland and finally the entire New York-Chicago routes were opened. The flying of the first-class mail by air, wherever possible, at the 2¢ rate, was begun on July 18, 1919. The Chicago-Omaha, Omaha-San Francisco and, ultimately, the entire daytime Columbia transcontinental route was initiated. Feeder routes to serve the Columbia mail were developed, that is, Minneapolis-Chicago and St. Louis-Chicago. The first pioneer day and night test flights from New York to San Francisco were flown on February 21, 1921.

Otto Praeger was a man who loved the airmail and the pilots and mechanics who made it go. His most treasured accomplishment of all was the transcontinental airmail, and he, more than any other single person, was the man who made it happen. It was the culmination of a dream for him — a dream that he had told Ben Lipsner about in 1918. Praeger said, "Airmail is here to stay, and we've got plans to expand the service clear across the country." Otto Praeger literally made his own dream come true.

Chapter 3

The Mystery of 38262

How did the number 38262, which appears on the first airmail stamp, Scott C3, also show up on the actual plane that took off from Washington, D.C., on May 15, 1918, with this nation's first organized airmail? This number

The Jenny on this 24¢ airmail stamp of 1918 carries the number 38262, the number of the plane that made the first flight out of Washington, D.C.

coincidence is made even more unusual by these historical assumptions:

• Most authorities agree that the stamp itself was hurriedly put together and printed prior to May 9, 1918.

• The planes themselves were not ordered by Major Reuben Fleet until May 6 and could not have been specially produced much before May 12 to 14. By this time, the stamp already had been printed, since its first day of issue was May 13, 1918.

• No records could be found that indicated any prior planning as to the number. Fleet himself recalled no such coordinating maneuvers between plane and stamp.

How then did the plane number get on the stamp when the plane wasn't even off the assembly line when the stamp was printed? The story of the first airmail flight was told by Philip H. Ward in a stamp paper, *Philatelic News*, dated March 1931.

Ward, pioneer dealer and originator of much airmail material, said, "The illustration of the airplane used in this article was taken by the Signal Corps shortly before

Boyle takes off in Jenny 38262, heading the wrong direction.

its first flight as an airmail carrier and was used by the Bureau of Engraving and Printing as a model in designing the 24¢ stamp." The picture with Ward's article shows Curtiss Jenny 38278, the plane that Torrey Webb used on the New York-Philadelphia run on that first day.

Ward had to have been quite wrong in that assumption. The picture could not have been taken shortly before the first flight and appear on a stamp that quickly. Even as speedily as Henry Goodkind thought that Scott C3 was designed and printed, that time schedule taxes our credulity too much, notwithstanding the fact that this plane carried the wrong number.

There is wide speculation as to just how long this stamp was in the design development stage. In his *Aeroplane News*, the famed A.C. Roessler said that "the design was approved May 10 in two colors, red and blue, but was not ready in time for the first trip." Of course, Roessler was wrong, and the stamp was ready for the first flights.

A copy of a Washington newspaper piece dated March 3, 1918, read: "The Post Office Department is at work on designs for the new airmail stamps." Using that dateline of March 3, the phrase "is at work on the designs" puts the initial development of this stamp much earlier than Goodkind, Ward, Fleet, Roessler and many others had presumed. It, of course, can be argued what "at work on designs" means.

To me that newspaper statement makes sense and is probably correct when you consider one important fact. The original date set for the beginning of the airmail was April 15, not May 15. This reinforces the story of earlier design work. Such an earlier starting date on the stamp makes sense when the original April 15 starting date is transposed into the whole stamp flight timetable. Assuming that the stamp was under development in March and not hurriedly assembled before the May 1 trip, the agreement of the plane and stamp numbers would seem to call for even more planning and coordination.

What really happened between the Post Office Department, the Signal Corps, the Bureau of Engraving and

Printing, the Aerial Mail Service and that Curtiss plant in Long Island? How did George Boyle get to fly with the same number on both his plane and his mail? Major D.C. Peebles presented what to me was the final and most conclusive answer to this numbers puzzle. The major had access to the archives of the Air Force for a short time and looked up some old correspondence that bears directly on the issue at hand.

Peebles' first clue is a memo to Major Fleet, Air Service Division, dated May 8, 1918: "This confirms our telephone conversation of 6 May. You are advised that the

New York Postmaster Thomas G. Patten hands the mailbag to Lieutenant Torrey Webb, who prepares to fly plane 38278 out of Belmont Park racetrack on Long Island.

last of the 12 planes for use in connection with the U.S. Aero Mail Service will ship from the Curtiss plant midnight Sunday./ signed/ R.M. Jones, Equipment Division." Now here is some new data. Fleet said that he picked up some of the planes and that he ordered six from Colonel Deeds. This memo states that 12 planes were specially modified and mentions delivery, not pick up, though Fleet may well have picked up the first six piece-meal, as he states in *Fifty Years of Air Mail.*

The second discovery that Major Peebles made in those archives is unfortunately not dated — nor are the copies with it. It is a simple requisition form listing the numbers of all 12 airmail planes. The lists (originally in two columns) read as follows: Washington-Philadelphia 38262, 38274, 38275, 38276, 38277, 38278; Philadelphia-New York 39362, 39363, 39364, 39365, 39366, 39367. One outstanding deviation in these lists is at once appar-ent, if you look at the numbers closely. All of the plane numbers in each of the two separate groups are in numer-ical sequence — except for 38262.

It would seem obvious now that the Equipment Divi-sion of the Air Service Division withheld 38262 from normal sequential plane assignment. There had to be a reason for doing that, and the only one that makes sense is that the designers or the Bureau of Engraving and Printing asked for a number to use on the Jenny stamp vignette and were given 38262. Probably the Post Office Department or someone in the Aerial Mail Service asked that that number be withheld and assigned to the Wash-ington mail plane. And so, "38262" appeared on both the stamp, which was designed earlier than May, and the plane, which was not built until a mere two or three days ahead of the first flight.

Incidentally, Major Peebles said that the records show that old number 38262 flew for at least the following year of 1919 but that Boyle's name shows up on no further flights. Stamp collectors know that Boyle did make one more flight, but it was a last-chance trial with Major Fleet. Boyle failed it.

Chapter 4

The Planes

One of the first and, by all odds, the most famous of the early aircraft to carry the United States mail was the Jenny. Made by Curtiss and officially known as the JN4H, she was primarily a military plane and woefully lacking in many respects for carrying mail. The Jenny's load capacity, over and above the pilot's weight, was only about 160 pounds. She was powered by an Hispano-Suiza engine, which was rated at just 150 horsepower. The engine was water-cooled and of the high-compression type. Thus, Jenny was a high-altitude aircraft somewhat unsuited to the early pilots' needs to fly low to better follow rivers, railroad tracks, and other ground reference points. Of major concern also was her limited fuel capacity — just 21 gallons, about as much as an automobile holds.

These drawbacks of the Curtiss Jenny and other similar early planes demanded a sort of seat-of-the-pants flying technique. It called for pilots who were not afraid, when necessary, to set the plane down in cornfields, scrub brush, meadows, or wherever they were when the gas ran low or the radiator overheated.

Much of the Jenny's notoriety is really undeserved. She was used at first only on the Washington-to-Philadelphia leg of the original airmail route. On the New York-to-

Philadelphia portion, the slightly more powerful Curtiss R-4s were used. While they are seldom heard of, the R-4 planes were in the air just as early and just as often as the more famous Jenny. Nevertheless, it is the Jenny whose image appears on the first three United States airmail stamps. If you will get out your magnifying glass and look at the planes closely on any of the three issues, you will see a faint number — 38262 — on the fuselage. This was the exact number on the plane used in the first planned

The Jenny 38262 appears on this 10¢ airmail stamp issued in 1968 to mark the 50th anniversary of the United States Airmail Service.

flight from Potomac Park, Washington, D.C. I say "planned" because the flight was aborted by an emergency landing at Waldorf, Maryland. As a sidelight of interest, when the 10¢ airmail of 1968 was issued honoring the 50th anniversary of that first flight, the Jenny on that stamp was such an exact duplicate of the original that the same number appears on the side of the fuselage.

Another early carrier was the Standard JR1B. This craft had a larger load capacity, 180 pounds; a more powerful engine, 180 horsepower; and a greater range than the Jenny. The Standard was the ship used in the first New York-Chicago through service begun September 5, 1918. As a philatelic image, she remains anonymous. The only other airplane shown on those first six airmail stamps was the DeHavilland DH-4, on the 24¢ issue of 1923. Her philatelic recognition was five years late. The DeHavilland also was used as an airmail carrier in that first year of operation. Powered by the famous Liberty 400-horsepower motor, the DeHavilland had a range of 350 miles initially. Just as important, as later models were improved, the Liberty engines operated more satisfactorily at low levels than either the Curtiss Jenny or the Standard. It was the DH-4 that was used as the longer flight legs of the transcontinental routes developed.

In fiscal 1921, the Post Office paid plane manufacturers $476,000 for new planes and for the remodeling of Army aircraft. This reworking of military planes was stopped on July 1 of that year when the DeHavilland was declared the official United States mail plane. It won that role because it was fast, reliable, easily repaired, durable and could carry 500 pounds of payload. This was the craft flown cross-country from New York to San Francisco and actually was the ship that sent the airmail service winging over the whole United States.

Some other early aircraft, with their dates of first use and primary routes, were: Martin twin-engine (Cleveland to Chicago, 1924); Douglas M-2 (Los Angeles to Salt Lake City, 1926); Curtiss Carrier Pigeon (New York to Chicago, 1926); Ryan monoplane (Seattle to Los Angeles, 1926); Swallow mail plane (Elko, Nevada, to Pasco, Washington, 1926); and Waco B-9 biplane (Pittsburgh to Cleveland, 1927).

Much more vital to the growth of airmail than these machines were the men who flew them. Operating with what, in the main, were inadequate aircraft with no radio communication for the first two years, with under-powered engines and very short flying-range limits, these intrepid "hedgehoppers" created, by raw nerve, an airmail service that went from 218 miles long to 3,000 miles long in just two short years.

Otto Praeger, second assistant postmaster general, commented on the New York-to-Chicago route opened in

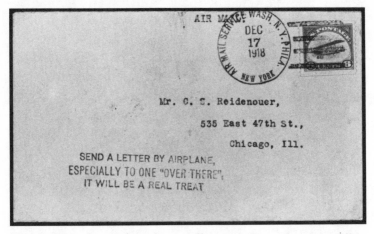

"Send a letter by airplane,/especially to one 'over there'; it will be a real treat" is the message on the handstamped cachet. This cover was flown on the experimental service on the New York City-Cleveland-Chicago route on December 18, 1918.

1919: "Very few people realize what an undertaking this is. Never has a trip by air been undertaken whereby a ship leaves for an 800-mile voyage — flying over mountains with few landing places — an undertaking which, six months ago, would have been regarded as an impossibility. When you consider it is being done with a single engine plane, the task is stupendous."

"Stupendous" is the precise word for those early pilots. To mention a few, they were: J.C. Edgerton, Walter Miller, Torrey Webb, E.W. Kilgore, Stephen Bonsal, H.P. Culver, Ed Gardner, Max Miller, Robert Shank, and

M.A. Newton. Drawing salaries of from $3,000 to $5,000 yearly, they literally put their lives on the line every day to build a service that most of the public did not use — much less appreciate. Kilgore, for example, went down five times. Walt Miller crashed four times, as did Stephen Bonsal. As important as their contributions were, the real builders of the airmail service were not the adminstrators, or the plane manufacturers, or even Lipsner and Praeger, who began it all. The real creators of the airmail were those few brave pioneer pilots who climbed out of their downed and damaged airplanes and took off again and again and again.

Chapter 5

The Preparations

The events leading up to the start of the United States airmail on May 15, 1918, spread over several departments of the government and involved some frantic scrambling for those charged with getting it off the ground. A chronology of those times is best viewed on a day-by-day basis:

Early 1918: President Wilson's cabinet discussed plans for an airmail service. They called for bids from the private sector, but none was forthcoming. When bids did not materialize, Colonel E.A. Deeds of the Aircraft Production Board suggested that the training gained in a mail service would be valuable for Army pilots. He proposed that the Army fly the new airmail. Wilson agreed, issued a statement to that effect and proclaimed that "America will win the war with aviation."

March 1, 1918: On this date an agreement was signed jointly by the War Department and the Post Office Department to operate the airmail. Congress had appropriated $100,000 for the new venture.

May 2, 1918: Colonel Henry Damm and Major Oscar Brindley were killed testing the first Liberty engine installed in a DeHavilland DH-4 at South Field in Dayton, Ohio. Major Reuben Fleet, who was appointed officer in charge of the Aerial Mail Service, and others inspected the wreckage. The cause of crash was blamed on a spark plug dropped on a lower wing, probably by a mechanic. This plug apparently had rolled back into a gap between wing and aileron, which caused the jamming of the

Major Reuben Fleet was appointed officer in charge of the United States Aerial Mail Service in 1918.

plane's banking control mechanism. Fleet test-flew another DH-4, and it performed well. The Damm-Brindley accident was judged a freak occurrence, and the DH-4s ultimately joined the ranks of airmail craft.

May 3, 1918: The War Department ordered its Air Service arm to start the airmail between Washington and New York each way every day except Sunday. Planes were to depart both terminals at 11 a.m. beginning Wednesday, May 15, with intermediated landing and mail service at Philadelphia. The air line distance between the two cities was 218 miles. The order was given by Newton D. Baker, secretary of war, at the behest of President Woodrow Wilson. Upon the recommendation of Colonel H.H. Arnold, Major Fleet was appointed officer in charge of Aerial Mail Service in addition to his other pilot training duties.

May 6, 1918: Secretary Baker called Fleet to his office for a meeting. Fleet reported that the air service had no planes capable of flying non-stop from Washington to Philadelphia or from Philadelphia to New York. He asked Baker for more time to get some Curtiss JN4H Jennies outfitted with double gas capacity, a hopper for mail pouches and dual controls. Postmaster General Albert Burleson was summoned to Baker's office. Burleson flew into a rage at Fleet's requests for delay. The press already had been told that the aerial mail would begin May 15. "It has to start then," said Burleson, "even if war work suffers." Baker agreed with Burleson. He saw the promise to the press as the crucial point and felt that the War Department had to force the start of the airmail even if pilots had to land in open fields en route.

Fleet called Deeds from Baker's phone and asked him to get six Jennies from the Curtiss plant at Garden City, Long Island. These ships were to have a mail hopper and double gas and oil reserves. They were to be delivered to Mineola Air Field by May 14. The Curtiss plant interrupted the production of war-training planes to get the special order. They installed two regular 19-gallon fuel tanks and two regular 2½-gallon oil tanks, hooking them together for a common feed. The normal range of the Jenny with just one gas tank was a mere 88 miles. This is what Fleet meant when he said originally that the Army training ships couldn't make it between the cities of Washington, Philadelphia and New York.

Fleet then phoned August Belmont, a friend who

owned the Belmont race track on Long Island. Belmont agreed to let the new Aerial Mail Service use the infield of his race track as the New York terminus of the airmail. Fleet arranged for the race track to be used as the terminus because he did not want to interrupt regular Army pilot training then going on at Mineola Field.

May 13, 1918: Fleet and five other pilots — Culver, Webb, Miller, Bonsal and Edgerton — went to the Curtiss factory. Pilot Boyle stayed in Washington. Webb was to fly one Jenny with mail to Bustleton Field in Philadelphia on "opening day." Edgerton and Culver were sent to Philadelphia with two mail planes. Edgerton was to fly the relay mail into Washington with Culver relaying the Washington mail into New York. It is interesting to note here that Boyle and Edgerton — the two pilots "politically appointed" — were scheduled to handle mail both in and out of Washington, D.C.

May 14, 1918: The two mail planes flown to Philadelphia were in such poor condition that Fleet, Edgerton and Culver spent most of this night working on the engines and airframes. They even discovered a hole the size of a pencil in one gasoline tank. In the middle of the night, they plugged it up with a plain old bottle cork.

May 15, 1918: One of the two Philadelphia planes was pronounced ready to fly at about 8 a.m. Fleet flew it into Washington, arriving at Potomac Park's Polo Grounds at about 10:30 a.m. Lieutenant Boyle was scheduled to take off just 25 minutes later. According to Fleet's memoirs, Lipsner failed in his assignment to have aviation gasoline available at Potomac Park. Some delay was encountered from a British aircraft and two American planes before the airmail could begin. Boyle finally took off in Jenny 38262. Meanwhile, Webb and Edgerton were flying Jenny 38278 successfully from New York to Philadelphia and from Philadelphia to Washington.

Chapter 6

'Wrong-Way' Boyle

The day was Wednesday, May 15, 1918. The place was the Polo Grounds, just outside Washington, D.C. The occasion was the first official transportation of United States postcards and letters by airplane. Letters and even parcels had been carried by air in this country as early as 1911 — occasionally with the sanction of the Post Office Department but never before with a specially issued stamp and very rarely with a planned route and schedule.

The plane to fly the first leg between Washington and Philadelphia had been flown to Potomac Park early that day. By correct designation, it was a Curtiss JN4H — an Army training plane whose front cockpit had been removed and replaced with webbing to carry the mail sacks. By a more affectionate and well-known designation, it was a "Jenny."

Benjamin Lipsner, superintendent of airmail, and Otto Praeger, second assistant postmaster general, were waiting to see if Woodrow Wilson, the president of the United States, would show up in time for the take-off scheduled for 10:30 a.m. Wilson and other dignitaries had been invited, but there had been no firm commitment by the president. Finally, just a few minutes before 10:30, President Wilson arrived along with Postmaster General Albert S. Burleson and other officials. Embarrassingly enough, the ground crew and Lieutenant George Boyle, the first flight pilot, could not get the Jenny's engine to turn over. For several minutes the crew spun the propeller by hand. Lipsner later said that the pilot flying the plane to the Polo Grounds had reported a nearly full fuel-gauge reading while in flight. A quick examination, however, revealed a need for gasoline, and the plane was refueled. The engine caught, and all was in readiness for Boyle's take-off at approximately 10:50, some 20 minutes behind schedule.

President Wilson had brought something with him to the first-flight ceremonies. It was a letter addressed to

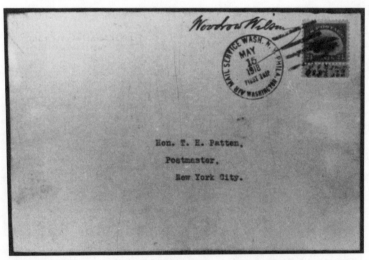

Woodrow Wilson's signature alongside the stamp and the initials of six postal officials on its selvage created this first-trip cover that sold for $1,000 at an auction to benefit the Red Cross.

Postmaster Patten of New York City. Wilson had canceled the 25¢ carmine and blue stamp by signing his name across its face. This cover was destined for a Red Cross benefit auction being held in New York. There it was to be sold for charity for $1,000.

Boyle was to fly to Bustleton Field near Philadelphia. His mail was to be turned over to Lieutenant Harry Culver, who would fly the second leg with a fresh plane from Philadelphia to New York, landing at Belmont Park racetrack, the most suitable airfield available. Boyle was carrying about 140 pounds of mail — 300 letters for Philadelphia, 3,300 for New York City, and 3,000 for destinations beyond New York to be forwarded by regular mail — plus, of course, the presidential cover. All of this added up to a gross revenue for the Post Office of $1,584.

With the Army flying the planes and the Post Office in charge of the new service, the first airmail schedule called for one flight north and one south each day except Sun-

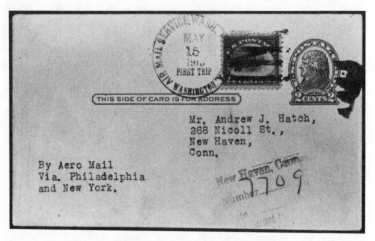

Lieutenant George Boyle carried this postal card on his ill-fated flight of May 15, 1918, out of Washington, D.C.

day. The schedule was to be as follows: Southbound: leave New York noon, arrive Philadelphia 1:10 p.m.; leave Philadelphia 1:25 p.m., arrive Washington 3:20 p.m. Northbound: leave Washington 11:30 a.m., arrive Philadelphia 1:15 p.m.; leave Philadelphia 1:30 p.m., arrive New York 2:30 p.m. A different pilot and airplane flew each leg of the schedule, changing at Philadelphia. Thus, each day, except Sunday, four pilots and four planes were flying the route.

But let's get back to our first pilot, Lieutenant Boyle. Lipsner puts the description of that first flight like this. The following is a paraphrase of the substance of Lipsner's recollection: "The president and the postmaster general delighted us all with their presence. Though the flight was somewhat late in getting off, the plane lifted beautifully, and Lieutenant Boyle took off into a clear Maryland sky. The crowd at the airport applauded and smiled happily. As Lieutenant Boyle banked his plane and headed into his flight pattern, I was probably the only one in the crowd not cheering. My heart sank. Boyle was headed in the wrong direction — straight south."

Boyle ended up in a forced landing at Waldorf, Maryland, lost and off course due to what he later said were compass problems. The airmail was loaded into a truck and driven back to Washington. Lieutenant Culver waited in vain in Philadelphia for cargo that did not arrive. It was held over until Thursday and flown with that day's dispatch. The glorious beginnings of the airmail had ended ingloriously. The 6,600 letters and cards wound up in a truck. The loud and numerous critics of the airmail had a field day. As for Boyle, he went back to flying for the Army after one or two additional flights. His name is not found on the list of the Army pilots who carried on.

Chapter 7

The Politics

Somewhere back in the simpler days of my youth, I heard a phrase that has stuck with me these many years: "He who ignores politics is a fool, for politics will surely not ignore him." Few will disagree that political manuevers and pressures are everywhere today. Few may remember, however, that these conditions were no less true for Reuben Fleet, Ben Lipsner, Otto Praeger and other early founders of the United States airmail. They had to play the political game continually with Congresses, presidents and a general public who never seemed satisfied with the progress of airmail development in the teens and twenties of this century.

Though politicians have always tried to interdict in the operations of the airmail and postal system, I will concentrate only on the Wilson and Harding years. These represent by no means, however, the only instances of airmail politicking. Major Reuben H. Fleet once was asked why President Wilson was so determined to start an airmail service literally in the middle of a major war. Why was personnel and equipment that might have been needed in the 1918 all-out war effort assigned to the new airmail service? Fleet, who commanded the early Army mail pilots, replied that "it was difficult for him to fathom." He speculated that President Wilson felt that carrying the mail would be good training for United States aviators. Fleet did not feel that Wilson attached any real significance to the long-range potentials of the air service itself.

Four well-trained and capable Army pilots were chosen. Then Lieutenant George Leroy Boyle was picked.

Two presidents who had great influence on early United States airpost. Woodrow Wilson, shown on the 17¢ stamp, began it in the middle of a war. Warren Harding's threat to end it caused the untimely transcontinental flights that brought glory to Jack Knight. Harding is portrayed on the 2¢ stamp.

Selecting Boyle was perhaps the first airmail political appointment. He was engaged to marry the daughter of one Judge McChord, whose legal decisions had saved the Parcel Post System in the courts. Post Office Department officials were determined to show their political gratitude.

Boyle took off with the first airmail from Washington on May 15, 1918. He proceeded to get lost, crashed in a field in Maryland and thoroughly botched the first airmail attempt. Fleet said that the Post Office insisted that Boyle be given a second chance, even after that first inglorious performance. Fleet accompanied Boyle in a separate training plane nearly half way to Philadelphia on his second mail flight to "ensure his being on course." After

Fleet's plane left him, Boyle still ended up near the mouth of the Potomac — lost again.

According to Fleet, the Post Office Department requested that "Lieutenant Boyle be given a third chance, and if he failed, the department would take responsibility for his failure." Major Fleet replied: "Your request is denied. Lieutenant Boyle has not had sufficient training to be entrusted with aerial mail and is being sent for further instruction by the Aviation Section of the Signal Corps. If the Postmaster General wants the Aerial Mail Service to be put in proper light before the public, he will announce to the press that the Army in charge of the service had no voice in Boyle's selection." Fleet's firm stand ended the short airmail career of the hapless Boyle, his fiancee and her politically important father notwithstanding.

Politics also entered into the choice of Lieutenant James Edgerton as an early Army mail pilot. At the time of his selection, his father was the purchasing agent of the Post Office Department. However, this was a happier example of pressure politics. Edgerton, who had the proper qualifications, turned out to be one of the airmail service's best fliers. Fleet was quite complimentary about Second Assistant Postmaster General Otto Praeger: "He backed me in every recommendation we made."

Fleet was less than happy with Postmaster General Albert Burleson. "He was often announcing to the press the mighty things we were going to do without consulting us," said Fleet.

As the airmail expanded west, not all of the mail was really going by plane. At one time, it was flown from New York to Chicago in the daylight hours, put on trains from Chicago to Cheyenne at night and flown on the second morning from Cheyenne to San Francisco. Other more complex schedules were later developed involving trains and planes between different points, but the end result was the same. This combined plane-train system cut the transcontinental mail time to 42 hours coast to coast in 1920 — about half the time needed via rail alone. That wasn't good enough to satisfy some members of Congress and a presidential candidate named Warren G. Harding.

In his campaign speeches promising greater economy in government, candidate Harding had promised to save money by grounding the new airmail system unless it flew day and night to realize its full time-saving potential. Harding was elected over James Cox and was scheduled to take office in March 1921. The Post Office had to do something dramatic to get public opinion behind the new airmail before Harding assumed the presidency, or its days were surely numbered. Thus were born, out of political expediency, the trial coast-to-coast flights of February 22 and 23, 1921.

They were potentially disastrous as far as many airmail officials were concerned. To try such an experiment in the worst possible time — the middle of a severe midwestern winter — was against all good sense and reason. Nevertheless, two planes left New York flying west, and two departed San Francisco going east on February 22. Politics had won out over good judgment and also over extremely bad weather conditions. Pilot W.F. Lewis crashed and was killed near Elko, Nevada, on one of the eastbound flights. Of the two westbound planes that left New York, one crash-landed in Pennsylvania and the second got no further west than Chicago.

Chapter 8

First Successful Flight

I have practically ignored the pilot who flew the very first successful airmail flight on May 15, 1918. Other than a passing mention, little has been said about Torrey Webb — an American airmail stalwart who deserves better. Back in the early 1900s, this delightful and outgoing gentleman stumbled into the airmail business somewhat against his will.

Torrey Webb enlisted in the Army during World War I and was assigned to the Signal Corps where he learned to fly. He was commissioned a lieutenant, and he wanted to use his new flying skills to fight Germans. When Lieutenant Webb was ordered to join the six Army fliers designated to carry airmail on the new New York-Washington route, his reaction was less than enthusiastic. "I didn't want any part of it," he said. "I told my commanding officer I didn't come into the service to waste time flying any mail."

Despite Webb's protests, Major Reuben Fleet ordered Webb to join those other Army fliers who were to become the first airpost pilots: Edgerton, Kilgore, Bonsal, Culver and Boyle. Webb didn't like it, but like any good soldier, he took the job and complained no more.

On May 15, 1918, a small crowd gathered at Belmont

Park in Long Island to watch Webb take off with the first mail in the world that was part of a permanent, scheduled airmail system. His route was New York to Philadelphia. The plane was to take off at 11:30 that morning. Torrey Webb was used to following schedules and to him 11:30 meant 11:30. The mere fact that the last of a coterie of

Lieutenant Torrey Webb (right) receives a good-luck horseshoe from French flier Henri Farre just before taking off on May 15, 1918, from Belmont Park raceway. Webb's flight was to be the first successful airmail run on a permanent, scheduled airmail system.

speakers was still orating at that time did not daunt Webb at all. Precisely at 11:30 he climbed into the cockpit and "gave her the gun" — speaker or no speaker. The nonplused official tried in vain to finish his talk as the engines of the Jenny drowned his last few words.

Torrey Webb made the 90-mile flight to Philadelphia in exactly one hour, turning his 144-pound mail load over to Edgerton at Bustleton Field. At that time, he did not know that he had just completed the first successful airmail flight. (Lieutenant George Boyle had taken off from Washington prior to Webb at 10:50 a.m., but Boyle ended up on his back near Waldorf, Maryland — off course. The Boyle mail was forwarded by truck.)

Webb's load consisted of 2,457 covers plus many assorted packages and a substantial amount of newspapers. Thus, the May 15 New York covers might be termed the

Torrey Webb signed this cover, which was carried on his New York-to-Philadelphia flight on May 15, 1918.

very first flight letters of that auspicious postal day to make it from origin to destination.

About a month later, after the French pilot Vannelle had crashed on take-off, Webb was summoned to fly the mail on Postmaster General Burleson's ill-planned new route from New York to Boston. This trip turned into an aerial nightmare. "The weather was awfully bad, and that flight to Boston was a 'dinger,' " said Torrey Webb. "It was raining cats and dogs when I got to the landing strip. They had marked out an old race track near Boston, and the track was covered with holes that they had filled in with ashes." As Webb's plane landed, the landing gear hit some of those chuckholes and broke in two. The aircraft flipped over on its back, but Webb emerged unhurt.

The return trip to New York some days later was a "dinger" too, said Torrey. "Visibility was zero-zero, and I just skimmed over the telephone poles all the way." With that New York-Boston fiasco behind him, Webb decided to get out of both the Army and airmail flying. "I had had it," he said. He left the Army in March 1919 with the rank of captain.

Webb had been a mining student at Columbia University in New York prior to his Army service. "Mining was at a low ebb when I quit the Army, so I got into the nearest thing to it, and that was oil." He worked the Texas oil fields for a while and then moved to California where the small company he joined in 1922 was later acquired by the Texas Company (Texaco). Webb moved up the management line in the oil business and, in November 1941, was named a vice president of Texaco, responsible for all of that company's operations in eight western states.

Webb was also an ardent fan of, and a financial contributor to, the University of Southern California in his later years. USC dedicated a building that houses 328 students and faculty members. They named it Webb Towers. the top floor and a pair of binoculars for a free seat."

His friends maintain that Torrey Webb was a remarkable man — a man who gave his best to the airmail, the oil business and USC. Torrey Webb died November 29, 1975. He was 82. At his request, he was buried at sea.

Chapter 9

Airmail Pilot No. 1

Major Reuben Hollis Fleet — the man who commanded those first six Army lieutenants who flew the mail
from May to August 1918 — was a tall, broad-should-
ered, imposing man who, back in 1918, had no desire to
get involved with the beginnings of the aerial mail service. His Army job was executive officer to Colonel Henry H. "Hap" Arnold. His responsibility was the training
of pilots for war at some 34 different flying installations.

A War Department directive of May 3, 1918, was to
change his life and push him against his will into becoming an airmail great. That directive commanded the air
service to inaugurate airmail flights between Washington
and New York in 12 days. It wasn't until May 6, when
Secretary of War Newton D. Baker summoned Fleet to
his office, that the major learned that his boss, "Hap"
Arnold, had recommended him for the task of getting the
airmail off the ground.

Fleet had just nine days until take-off and hurriedly
arranged for modifications to the JN4H Jenny planes under construction at the Curtiss plant in Long Island. He
also talked a friend, August Belmont, into permitting him
to use the Belmont race track as the New York landing
field. Fleet made no bones about not liking his new job.

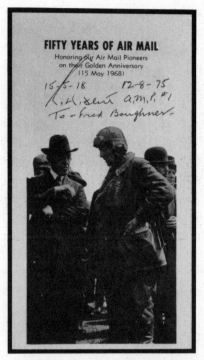

On May 15, 1918, President Wilson greeted Major Reuben Fleet a few minutes after Fleet landed the Jenny that Boyle was to use for the Washington-to-Philadelphia flight. This pamphlet honoring 50 years of United States airmail is signed by Fleet.

He especially did not like the rush schedule that Postmaster General Burleson had laid down and already disseminated to the press. But, like it or not, he got the job done.

His principal concern, next to planes "that couldn't even fly non-stop from New York to Philadelphia," was the selection of capable pilots. They were none too plentiful in those early days. Fleet was furious when he learned that he was going to get to pick just four out of the anticipated six. The Post Office Department told him that it would choose the other two.

Fleet's personal choices were Lieutenants Torrey Webb, Walter Miller, Howard Culver and Stephen Bonsal. The Post Office saddled him with George Boyle and James Edgerton. I have noted previously that the hapless Boyle was engaged to a judge's daughter whose verdict had saved the Parcel Post System. Edgerton was the son of the Post Office Department's purchasing agent. Fleet was quickly getting his nose rubbed in "practical politics" as performed in high places. Up to the very end of his life, Fleet continued to resent the Boyle incident and continued to write about it in letters.

Fleet also refused to believe the allegation of President Wilson that the airmail was being started in the midst of a

The United States Post Office Department took over operation of the airmail from the Signal Corps on August 12, 1918. This flight cover is franked with a 16¢ airmail stamp.

war to give training to potential wartime fighter pilots. Some of Fleet's later correspondence also revealed that he personally doubted that Wilson had any sound long-range concepts of airmail growth. Though I never met Major Fleet in person, I had the privilege of corresponding with him occasionally over the last few years of his life. He

AIRMAIL PILOT NO. 1

seemed to me a most gracious man, always willing to answer a question or two, always prompt in his replies and very adept at expressing himself.

Reuben Fleet, judging from the articles he wrote and those personal letters that I received, was one of the more erudite of the early pioneers. The last letter I had from him is dated August 12, 1975. Somewhat ironically, it was on precisely that date 57 years earlier that the civilian pilots took over the flying of the mail from Fleet's Army personnel. Here are some of the things he had to say: "Replying to your letter of yesterday, the Second Assistant Postmaster General asked me, 'How much shall we charge for postage?' 'Is the idea to make the air service self-supported?' 'Yes,' replied Mr. Praeger. 'Is there a limit on the charge?' 'Yes, twenty-four cents,' said Praeger. 'Then I suggest twenty-four cents,' said I."

Fleet also maintained in that letter that it was Wilson himself, not Postmaster General Burleson, who asked that Lieutenant Boyle be the first air carrier. The resentment about that matter obviously was still there after 57 years. When the Post Office took over on August 12, Reuben Fleet went back to his training mission for "Hap" Arnold. When he left, however, he took with him something that no one else has or will ever have: the government's official designation as Airmail Pilot No. 1.

Reuben Fleet started his own aircraft company in 1923. He was an extremely successful businessman, and his company played a vital role in supplying planes for the American air victory over the Germans in World War II. In 1935, Fleet moved his Consolidated Aircraft Corporation to San Diego, where it later became the Convair Division of General Dynamics.

Fleet died on October 29, 1975, at the age of 88. His grave in Fort Rosecrans National Cemetary in San Diego overlooks the North Island Naval Air Station where he received his first training for his Army aviator's wings. When the major flew there, it was known as Rockwell Field. More than 250 persons attended the funeral service

Reuben Fleet (right) in later years as chairman of Consolidated Aircraft. With him is Joseph T. McNarney, head of Convair.

for the flying major.

He had many honors in his long lifetime, but perhaps one of the best came on November 22, 1975, less than a month after his death. He was named to the Aviation Hall of Fame in Dayton, Ohio. If we could ask him today which award he prized the most, I have my own idea as to what he would say. Fleet sent me a pamphlet in 1974. It is signed, "R.H. Fleet, A.M.P. No. 1."

Chapter 10

The Civilian Takeover

The Army pilots — six of them — who flew the first airmail under the direction of the Post Office Department, did not fly for long. From the day of that first flight on May 15, 1918, it was the intention of the Post Office to take over all operations of the service just as soon as possible. That takeover came on August 12, 1918, less than three months later. The Army flew the mail for just 87 days. The last Army pilots stepped out of their planes at New York and Washington on Saturday, August 10. The following Monday saw the service shed its khaki and

The first set of United States airmail stamps was issued in 1918 and featured the Curtiss Jenny. The values are 6¢, 16¢ and 24¢.

put on civilian clothes.

In those 87 days, the Army pilots flew 254 flights, covered about 29,500 miles, and experienced 16 forced landings. Their delivery and on-time record, considering the fields and aircraft, was amazingly good. On those final flights, J.C. Edgerton carried just 12 pounds of mail, Torrey Webb 15 pounds, E.W. Kilgore 7 pounds, and Webb again, on a second flight, 12 pounds. Remembering that the load capacities of the Jennies and R4s were approximately 160 pounds, it is readily apparent that the early airmail was not very popular. Records show that those early trips were carrying less than eight percent of their potential load. Assuming that cost might be a factor in

This flight cover is postmarked July 15, 1918, the first day of the new 16¢ rate implemented by the United States Post Office.

the disinterest of the general public, the postmaster general reduced the 24¢ rate to 16¢ for the first ounce, effective July 15, 1918. This 16¢ rate also included individual delivery service, as had the 24¢ rate. Thus, the 16¢ issue of 1918 was born.

In December of that year, the Post Office further reduced the rate to 6¢ for the first ounce, removing the immediate delivery proviso. This new regulation spawned the 6¢ issue of 1918.

Despite two reductions in seven months, the public was still apathetic toward sky mail, proving that cost was only a partial reason. For, though the Washington-Philadelphia-New York service had recorded on-time records, the schedule timing and the short 218-mile distance involved did not offer any real time-saving advantages over the planes' major competitor, the railway mail. If you had been a New York resident in 1918, your airmail letter posted on a Monday afternoon caught Tuesday's noon flight out of New York. The plane did not arrive in Washington until 3:20 p.m. — far too late for delivery until the following day. Result: Your airmail letter arrived not one hour faster than the regular post going by rail.

The new civilian operators of the Post Office Department quickly realized that airmail service along that short route would never have any real advantages over surface mail. They started to lay plans to go west to more distant

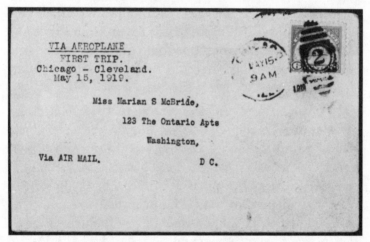

This cover was carried on the May 15, 1919, first Chicago-Cleveland flight. The route marked the establishment of the first leg of the transcontinental route.

delivery points — Cleveland, Chicago and the West Coast. It is a matter of record that the Post Office abandoned the original New York-Washington route entirely on May 31, 1921. Other short-flight mail-service routes from Chicago to Minneapolis (begun December 1, 1920) and from Chicago to St. Louis (begun August 16, 1920) also were scrapped in mid-1921.

The officials thus admitted that the airmail service was flying the wrong routes, and the real reason for public apathy was simply that, and not cost. Therefore, on May 15, 1919 — one year to the day after that first flight — a new airmail route was opened from New York to Cleveland. And, under this new plan, the airmail joined forces with its competition, the railroads. Cleveland became a "gateway" point. Airmail for the West was sent by plane to Cleveland, where it was placed aboard trains bound for Chicago and beyond. This shaved 16 hours off surface delivery from New York to the Midwest and 24 hours to the West Coast. Soon, it was apparent that Cleveland could be used as a "gateway" eastbound as well as westbound. Another airmail route was begun from Chicago to Cleveland. Mail flown on this route overtook a mail train bound for New York City and saved the same 16 hours on service from Chicago to the East Coast.

On these airmail routes operating in 1918 (New York-Cleveland, Cleveland-Chicago), there were eight mail planes in the air daily. According to Edward Keogh in his *History of Air Mail Service,* these planes flew 1,906 miles each day. Their performance record during the full year of 1919 was 96 percent plus. This record was attained despite the fact that "30 percent of these flights were made in rain, fog, mist or other conditions of poor visibility."

During this early time of civilian operation, when public usage was so low, the actual airmail hardly began to fill the sacks. Ben Lipsner, superintendent of the service, took the matter into his own hands. He wrote: "I couldn't bring myself to ask a pilot to take off in wind, rain and fog with just three or four pounds of airmail letters. So, we 'stuffed' the pouches full on several flights with regular mail to give the appearance of a full sack. Even the pilots themselves did not know this was going on."

On many flights, 90 percent of the payload was regular mail. Many a collector's 2¢ stamped cover is probably really a flight cover. It got a free plane ride in the effort of Lipsner and others to keep up pilot morale.

Chapter 11

The Controversy

In the beginning days of the United States airmail service, there were just the Curtiss R-4s and the Jennies. These planes, secured from the military by Ben Lipsner and Otto Praeger, flew the New York-Philadelphia and the Philadelphia-Washington routes. The need for a more suitable aircraft was soon apparent, however, and Lipsner spent much time with the Standard Aircraft Corporation of Elizabeth, New Jersey, working out the specifications on such a plane.

The result was the Standard mail plane. It had a mail-load capacity of 180 pounds, a 150-horsepower Hispano-Suiza engine, a speed of about 100 miles per hour and could climb to 6,000 feet in just 10 minutes. On August 6, 1918, six of the new Standards were delivered.

At the same time, Lipsner's Aerial Mail Service was dickering through Congress for some excess Handley-Page bombers. From 100 to 200 of these larger ships were thought to be available. It was the anticipated supply of these Handley-Pages that led the United States Post Office Department to try the New York-to-Chicago run via the experimental flights of Max Miller and Ed Gardner in September 1918.

The turnover of these Handley-Page machines was

never implemented, however, except for delivery of a very few. The Post Office Department finally despaired of ever getting its hands on enough of these promising-looking mail carriers. As Lipsner and others later learned, both the Jennies and the new Standards, each with 150-

More than 100 of these large Handley-Page bombers were supposed to be available to the United States Post Office. The Post Office wanted the bombers for the New York-to-Chicago run, but only a few ever materialized.

horsepower engines, had one insurmountable problem: It was impossible to buck a 40- to 50-mile-per-hour headwind with ships having a top speed of but 80 to 100 miles per hour. The Curtiss R-4s and the new DeHavilland DH-4s, on the other hand, had Liberty 400-horsepower engines and could cope with the storm elements much more successfully.

Lipsner put his money on these two planes and felt that they could adequately handle the needs of his new airmail service. His bosses in the Post Office Department — principally Second Assistant Postmaster General Otto Praeger — maintained that what the service needed was specially built aircraft or, at least, old aircraft completely remodeled. Praeger expressed the official Post Office position when he said, "A military plane is designed for military purposes, not mail or commerce. Its weight distribution is faulty when it comes to carrying letters, and the hope of the future is to have in the New York-to-Chicago service a machine provided with a distinct mail compartment."

Otto Praeger went on to recommend low compression engines, different fuselage design and strengthened land-

The DH-4s flew everywhere, including the coast-to-coast New York-to-San Francisco schedules.

ing gear. With many renovations and much reworking, Praeger felt that it might be possible to utilize some of the military equipment left over from World War I — but then and only then.

Fighting this position and taking Lipsner's side in Congressional debates on the issue was a young representative from New York, Fiorello LaGuardia, who had just resigned his air service commission. LaGuardia contended that the DH-4 was "the nearest to a perfect machine that was ever sent abroad." He said, "It should be an excellent machine to use for the transportation of mail at this time." The young New York Congressman went on to suggest that even the excess Jennies should continue to be used in routes such as New York-Philadelphia, Philadelphia-Washington and Omaha-Milwaukee. They would be "ideal planes for such short trips."

On December 15, 1918, the United States newspapers carried an announcement by Otto Praeger: The airmail service was to have special planes constructed or rebuilt at a cost of several million dollars. Lipsner, still convinced that regular military craft could do the job and being much opposed to opening a New York-Chicago route in the dead of winter, asked for a face-to-face meeting with Praeger.

Benjamin Lipsner had another bone in his throat. Praeger had made several appointments to the Aerial Mail Service that Lipsner highly disapproved of, and he had made them around Lipsner without any consultation with the superintendent of the airmail. Lipsner regarded many of these appointments as political in nature and the appointees as absolutely unfit for their positions.

At the meeting, Praeger told Lipsner quite firmly that the plans for new planes would go forward and that all appointments made by him would stand. Lipsner promptly resigned. Part of that resignation statement reads as follows: "In view of the announcement made today and the order issued by the Second Assistant Postmaster General (Praeger), I find it necessary to relinquish my position as first Superintendent of the Aerial Mail Service. When it is considered that, in one month, more than 11,000 miles of air travel is covered and thousands of letters carried, no further comments are necessary. I endeavored to maintain this high standard of efficiency by operating the service with the maximum of economy. This, I am sure, can be done with airplanes being turned over to the Post Office by the War Department without any extensive expenditures of public money . . ."

Max Miller, one of the airmail's ace fliers, quickly resigned in support of Lipsner. Fourteen more pilots on the New York-Washington run threatened to quit and disrupt the entire mail service. Some personal appeals — supposedly including one by Lipsner himself — prevented this very first pilots' strike and kept the mails flying.

Lipsner's position, though perhaps somewhat self-seeking, was vindicated to a degree at least when the Post Office Department announced on July 1, 1921, that the airmail service would henceforth use the DeHavilland DH-4 with the Liberty 12 engine as standard equipment. With heavier gears, larger pistons and better oil pumps, the new Liberty 12s proved reliable and dependable. The planes themselves, carrying up to 600 pounds of mail, seemed easy to maintain and long-lived. Of greatest importance, the records seemed to show that they were a safe aircraft as well. Thus, it turned out that both Lipsner and Praeger had been partially correct. The military DH-4s were successful, as Lipsner said they would be, but only after a new engine and other modifications had been added, as Praeger had said would be needed if new aircraft were not purchased.

The DH-4 was the principal plane used on all airmail routes in 1921. It was flying from New York to Washington, St. Louis to Twin Cities, New York to Cleveland, Cleveland to Chicago, Chicago to Omaha, Omaha to Salt Lake City, and Salt Lake City to San Francisco. There were other planes in use — Curtiss R-4s, Jennies, Martins and Junkers on certain lines — but only the DeHavilland was omnipresent. The DH-4, the workhorse of the early airmail and the ship that sent the mail winging from coast to coast, is the plane pictured on the 1923 24¢ airmail stamp. The plane continued in heavy use until 1926.

In May of that year, the first of 51 new Douglas mail planes began to be delivered. They had more than twice

The DH-4 was the principal plane used on all airmail routes in 1921. This cover was carried between Kansas City, Missouri, and Omaha on the first day of the American Legion Convention in Kansas City on October 31, 1921.

the load capacity of the DeHavilland and a great deal more speed. With the arrival of the Douglases, the age of the Jennies, the Curtisses, the Standards and the great DeHavillands came to an end. And with their passing, the age of airplane controversy ended also.

Chapter 12

The Promotion

A man may build the best proverbial mouse trap in the world, but if no one hears about it, what good is it? A postal service may develop the fastest new mail delivery on earth, but if nobody knows about it and uses it, what is its value? Those sentiments appear to reflect the operating maxims of the administrators and officials of the early airmail system in this country. Selling. Promoting. Merchandising. Public relations. Advertising. Just name the technique, and those first airmail leaders made use of it during the formative years of the new service — the decades of the 1910s, '20s and '30s. It was their job to sell a skeptical postal public on the safety, speed, reliability and convenience of the new airmail but at a higher price than regular domestic mail. When any service or product costs more than its competition, a planned promotional program becomes a necessity.

The selling of the airmail really began with the first flight from the Polo Grounds in Potomac Park near Washington, D.C., on May 15, 1918. One way to get the public's attention and plenty of newspaper space is to involve celebrities and an unusual gimmick. Both were used by the Post Office to mark the new airmail's first flight. Watching as Lieutenant Boyle took off for his disastrous trip in the wrong direction that morning were President and Mrs. Woodrow Wilson, Navy Secretary Josephus Daniels, Postmaster General Albert S. Burleson and a rather obscure assistant naval secretary named Franklin D. Roosevelt, along with members of the House and Senate committees on post office and post roads. Also on hand were leading officials of various aeronautical societies of the United States.

Those were the celebrities. What was the gimmick? It was a letter from Burleson to Postmaster Patten of New

"AIR-MAIL/SAVES TIME" is the
message on this meter.

York City with the new 24¢ airmail stamp canceled and autographed by President Wilson. To get some later additional publicity, the letter was to be auctioned off in New York City for the benefit of the American Red Cross. It sold for the minimum opening bid of $1,000. Thus was the selling of the airmail off and running.

The Post Office Department also realized that it had a built-in selling and advertising device through the use of postmarks and cachets. One of the stamp cancellation killers used widely in the early days read, "Airmail Saves Time." The words appeared in a box along with the picture of an early biplane. Special cachets were readied for almost every first or unusual flight. That first one from Potomac Park carried a round postmark enclosing the words, "Washington — Air Mail Service — Wash. N.Y. Phila. — May 15, 1918 First Trip." Even Burleson's ill-fated first try at a Boston-New York service got a special cachet reading, "Boston to New York," and in the double-circle postmark, "Boston, Mass. Air Mail June 9, 1918 First Trip." Other official cachets were made for the New York-Chicago flight on September 5, 1918; the transcontinental flights of July 1, 1924; the first New York-to-Chicago overnight airmail on July 1, 1925; and many others.

The Post Office appeared more than willing to cooperate with stamp shows, tying first days of issue and special cachets to many new airmail issues. Even the envelope became an airmail salesman. Use of special covers, with red and blue strips to highlight the airmail service, were

Issued circa 1934, four panes of four labels each were contained in booklets offered free to airmail users by the United States Post Office Department.

officially encouraged. Some of these envelopes even carried a special imprint that read, "Via Air Mail. Envelopes of this design approved by the P.O.D. for exclusive use in Air Mail."

The Post Office also distributed special booklets with airmail labels enclosed, fully gummed and separated by glassine-type paper. One of these was sent to me by Pat Herst and appears to have been issued about 1934 when the new 6¢ airmail rate had gone into effect with the debut of the 6¢ orange issue (Scott C19) on July 1 of that year. The cover reads, "Use Air Mail. Only 3¢ More," and shows a 3¢ stamp placed next to another three-center, which paid the first-class rate at that time. The real selling is inside the booklet where both front and back covers show such phrases as "Air Mail Travels Three To

"Use/Air Mail/Only 3¢ More" is the message on this United States booklet cover. On the back cover are the words "SPEED! SPEED! – AIR MAIL – SPEED! SPEED!"

Four Times Faster"; "Air Mail Schedules Are Co-Ordinated With Train Schedules"; "Air Mail May Be Sent Registered, Insured and C.O.D."; and "Distinctive Air Mail Stationery Will Assure Preferred Treatment." Inside the back cover are the words "SPEED! SPEED! — AIR MAIL — SPEED! SPEED!"

With the beginning of Contract Air Mail service, special large round cachets were provided not only for each flight but for each city along the CAM route. For example, when CAM 3 began on May 12, 1926, special town cachets were made for Dallas, Fort Worth, Oklahoma City, Wichita, Kansas City, St. Joseph, Moline and Chicago. A time-of-day designation also was printed within the cachet so that the CAM cover collector can follow the flight: 7 a.m. Dallas; 7:30 a.m. Fort Worth; 9:45 a.m. Oklahoma City; 1:45 p.m. Kansas City; and so on into Chicago. Even during the period of the so-called 2¢ airmail, from 1919 to 1924, the Post Office kept special airmail boxes in cities along the air routes and encouraged the public to place their letters therein for special airmail handling.

The late Charles Lindbergh probably was used more extensively than any other celebrity to promote the airmail. He signed several pictures of himself and his plane thusly: "I was proud to have done it for America. My reward will be your continued use of airmail." The pictures were distributed through the Post Office. Lindbergh also made a multitude of goodwill hops, courtesy flights and some first flights promoting airmail usage throughout Mexico, Guatemala, El Salvador, Panama, Bogota, San Juan and other Central American localities. The booklet pane covers of the Lindbergh airmail stamp of 1927 were advertisements in themselves. They pictured a map of all existing airmail routes and exhorted the public that "the airmail is the speediest means of transporting matter that has yet been devised. Its consistent use by the public will show a high percentage of time saved."

At one point, the Post Office even covered Douglas Fairbanks' flying jacket with airmail stamps and "mailed" him off in a plane. Many of the CAM private

With several United States 24¢ airmail stamps plastered on his flying jacket, actor Douglas Fairbanks Sr. was "airmailed" from Washington, D.C., to New York.

operators gave out baggage labels that were sold in sheets. One is from Robertson Aircraft Corporation, which flew CAM 2 from St. Louis to Chicago until 1928. The phrase at the top of the label waxes a little poetic: "On the Wings Of The Wind." Those are but a few of the promotion ideas used by the Post Office and others to convince a doubting-Thomas public to try the new airmail, even at higher postal cost. They seem to prove that early airmail postal officials were not about to keep their new "mousetrap" unsold, unpromoted and unadvertised.

Chapter 13

Heading West

During the crucial formative years of the American airmail system, this nation was not exactly blessed with the best of all postmasters general. In fact, from 1913 to 1921, that chair was held by a man whom recognized postal historians, such as Gerald Cullinan, have called "vain, coarse and arrogant." The eight years of this man's term have been dubbed "the most disastrous in the history of our postal establishment."

The man was Albert Sidney Burleson, and much of the real progress made under his administration was heartily opposed by this one-time Texas congressman. There was one development that Burleson wanted to see succeed, however, and that was his new Aerial Mail Department. So badly did he want it to succeed that he made a rash and untimely move once the New York-Washington airmail was off and flying.

The first official United States airmail service began on May 15, 1918. Just two weeks went by before Albert Burleson decided that he would expand the fledgling service to other parts of the country. On June 1, 1918 — a Saturday of all days — Burleson put out a surprise order to A.L. Hortung, chief of airmail operations at Belmont Park, Long Island. In the short span of that weekend,

Hortung was instructed to plan, equip and staff a New York-to-Boston airmail route by Monday, June 3. Burleson wanted it operational in just two days — and over a Saturday and a Sunday.

The flight from Mineola, New York, to Boston was delayed when the plane crashed on take-off. The mail was transferred from Mineola to the airfield at Belmont Park on Long Island on June 4, 1918, and flown to Boston on June 6 by Torrey Webb. This cover also carries an airmail backstamp of June 4, 1918, a previously unrecorded date for this backstamp.

Somehow Hortung managed to set up the first Boston flight from Aviation Field No. 1 at Mineola, Long Island, for 6 a.m., June 3, just as Burleson had ordered. The distinction of flying the first Boston mail went to a French Army officer, Lieutenant Gustave Vannelle. Mechanical problems delayed Vannelle until 9 a.m. When he did take off, he stabbed a wingtip into the muddy Mineo-

Landing at Saugus, Massachusetts, on June 6, 1918, Torrey Webb's Curtiss R-4 hit a runway pothole and upended. Five days later, Webb and the plane flew on to New York.

la field and crashed. Vannelle and his Irish mechanic, O'Brien, were only bruised, but the flight was scrubbed. The mail sacks were sent back to Belmont Park.

There, on Thursday, June 6, Lieutenant Torrey Webb, an experienced mail pilot with a perfect flight record, climbed into the air for a second try at the New York-Boston run. Webb's Curtiss biplane ran into bad weather immediately. This, along with compass trouble, forced him down near Saugus, Massachusetts, at a large estate belonging to one of the Boston Cabots. This field, like

Mineola, was soggy from heavy rains, and Webb's plane upended when it landed in a pothole. Webb was unhurt, but the craft and propeller were severely damaged.

The flight was scheduled to return to New York on June 9, but a delay in needed repair parts postponed it until June 11. That day also dawned rainy and foggy, but Webb left anyway. Flying almost blind and relying mainly on an uncertain compass, Webb finally landed at Belmont Park after more than three hours in the air and one

This cover received a "BOSTON-TO-NEW YORK" cancel along with a datestamp for the first Boston flight.

forced landing. That ended the abortive hurry-up try at establishing a New York-to-Boston mail segment.

The Post Office Department and Burleson decided to work on improving the New York-Washington route that was already a growing concern. Further plans to break the new airmail service out of that schedule were tabled for the rest of 1918.

In the first few months of 1919, a proposed transcontinental route was carefully laid out in four segments: New York-Cleveland; Cleveland-Chicago; Chicago-Omaha; Omaha-San Francisco. Wiser heads decided to try the

Cleveland-Chicago leg first. It was shorter than the Cleveland-to-New York jump, and it avoided flying over the dreaded "Hell Stretch" of the Allegheny mountains.

The inaugural Cleveland-Chicago run was flown on May 15, 1919, just one year after the first airmail flights. Pilot Trent Fry flew east from Chicago in a DH-4 Liberty — powered and carrying 31 pounds of airmail. Fry was to fly only as far as Bryan, Ohio, which had been set up as an interchange point. He made it to Bryan — 175 miles distant — in about two hours.

Meanwhile, pilot Ed Gardner had left Cleveland westbound for Bryan with nine pounds of airmail. He arrived at Bryan at the same time as Fry, about noon. Their mail was exchanged, and Fry flew back to Chicago with only six pounds of airpost but 249 pounds of regular, first-class mail. Gardner returned to Cleveland with Fry's original 31 pounds of airmail plus seven more. At this point, the railroads were handling the "airmail" from Cleveland to New York and vice-versa.

On July 1, 1919, the longer and more difficult New York-Cleveland portion was started. W.H. Stevens flew a DH-4 from Belmont Park to Bellefonte, Pennsylvania, where another pilot, E.F. White, and another DH-4 took the mail into Cleveland. This time there were six full pouches carried, and all of them held some 330 pounds of regular mail.

Pilot Ira Biffel, who was destined later to teach a young man named Charles Augustus Lindbergh to fly, carried the mail from Cleveland straight into Chicago. He had just four pounds of airmail but about 340 pounds of regular first-class mail. On the next day, July 2, a total of 43 pounds of airmail, but more than 750 pounds of first-class mail, was ferried both east and west over the three-lap course from New York to Chicago.

This nuts-and-bolts history of the early flying of first-class mail leads to this: With the success of the New York-Chicago routes, Postmaster Burleson was to make a ruling that, despite his many detractors, was at least a generation or so ahead of its time. It was a ruling that still starts debates among airmail specialists and postal historians today. In Burleson's judgment, the airlines at this early date should have carried all the mail, not just that franked with correct airmail postage. Accordingly, on July 18, 1919, the postmaster general issued a postal regulation that still prompts the question: Was there ever an official 2¢ airmail rate in the United States?

Chapter 14

The Mad Race

A few weeks after the first airmail flight — sometime in mid-summer of 1918 — Superintendent Ben Lipsner called a meeting of all his pilots and his chief mechanic, Eddie Radel. The purpose was to discuss routes, plans and personnel for a New York-Chicago try at establishing an airmail service between the then two largest cities in the United States. The pilots referred to the westward route over the Allegheny mountains as "Hell Stretch."

Late in August, pilots Max Miller and Ed Gardner were chosen to fly — at the same time, in two different planes — a route from New York City across the Alleghenies to Lock Haven, Pennsylvania, from Lock Haven to Cleveland, from Cleveland to Bryan, Ohio, and from Bryan into Chicago. Originally, it was hoped that both electrically heated flying suits and ground-to-air two-way radios would be available for the flights. Neither materialized in time, and the pilots had to rely on compasses and on ground telephones at their refueling stops to keep in touch with Lipsner.

From Lipsner's memoirs and other sources comes the following account of the Gardner-Miller maiden voyage. The two pilots were selected because they were among the best at their craft and both possessed a "sixth sense" at finding their way in bad weather conditions. A very real rivalry developed between them in the pre-flight days, each betting the other that he would be first into Chicago. At times, it is said, the feeling got so intense that Post Office officials had to intervene and pacify the two pilots. This, said Lipsner, is the spirit he wanted to engender — within reasonable bounds.

A coin flip decided that Miller should take off first. He was to fly alone. Gardner would follow and take with him the mechanic, Eddie Radel. The rationale here was that, should Miller have mechanical problems, Radel, following with Gardner, could handle them. At 7:08 on the

This cover was carried on the experimental flight by Max Miller and Ed Gardner from New York to Chicago via Lock Haven.

morning of September 5, 1918, Max Miller took off from Belmont Park, New York. He was to fly for the first two hours almost blinded by a heavy fog; he was using a 150-horsepower Standard ship.

Gardner's plane broke its tail skid in taxiing. Against the advice of Radel, he took another plane that had not even been flight tested. It happened to be a new Curtiss R-4 with a 400-horsepower engine.

But back to Miller. After flying for two hours in that fog, he thought he should be nearing Lock Haven, Pennsylvania. Carefully, he descended and broke into clear skies. He was safely over the mountains. Following a river for about a mile, he landed in what turned out to be Danville, Pennsylvania. After getting directions, he took off, flew for 45 minutes and reached his first stop — Lock Haven. He found that his radiator had sprung a leak. After refueling and making what on-the-spot repairs he could, he left Lock Haven about 11:45 a.m.

Gardner, meanwhile, had run into the same heavy weather and, with an unreliable compass, put down at Wilkes-Barre, Pennsylvania. He got on the phone to Lipsner, who was waiting in Chicago. His first words to Lipsner were, "Where's Max?" Gardner left Wilkes-Barre at 12:02 p.m., 17 minutes after Miller left Lock Haven. Gardner landed again in Bloomsburg, Pennsylvania, to get directions after flying through a violent rainstorm. Engine trouble forced him down once more at Jersey Shore, Pennsylvania, at 1 p.m. Finally, he made it to his first stop, Lock Haven, at 2:15 p.m., way behind schedule and with water and dirt in his gas line.

Now the second lap was on. Gardner knew Miller was somewhere ahead of him. Miller, having no idea where Gardner was, assumed that he was right on his tail. Early in the afternoon, Miller's engine began to overheat — the radiator problem again. He landed on the sloping side of a hill behind a farmhouse. An irritated farmer, brandishing a shotgun, shooed him off his property. Miller set down in another field a few miles away. Here, a friendlier farmer told him he was in "Jefferson." The farmer meant Jefferson County, Pennsylvania. Miller thought he meant Jefferson, Ohio, and flew a course that he thought would lead him to Cleveland.

The radiator continued to leak. Miller put down in a

third field, got some needed water and, at 4:25 p.m., land-ed at Cambridge, Ohio — far off course and 100 miles from Cleveland. He spent a couple hours working on the pesky radiator and, about 6 p.m., took off for Cleveland. Finally, at 8:30 p.m., he landed in a prairie seven miles outside that Ohio city.

After talking with Lipsner, Postmaster Murphy of Cleveland arranged for Miller to spend the night. The next morning Miller had to fly the Standard into the Glenn Martin Factory in Cleveland. The radiator was re-moved and repaired properly, but Miller did not get out of Cleveland until 2:15 p.m.

It was now September 6 — the second day of the mad, mad, mad race to Chicago. Gardner also had been marooned overnight (in Lock Haven) with mechanical woes and bad weather. At 10:45 a.m. on the second day, Gardner and Radel left Lock Haven with the clouds "hanging below the hill tops." Shortly after noon, Gardner landed in Sharpsville, Pennsylvania, to check his location. At 1:25 p.m., he sighted Lake Erie. At about this point, if Gardner had been able to find the Glenn Martin field, he would have seen an unusual sight — his rival Max Miller just taking off.

Gardner was on his way again about 4 p.m., now just 45 minutes behind Miller. The race was tightening up. Miller landed at Bryan, Ohio, at 4:25 p.m. and left within 30 minutes. Gardner also landed at Bryan — in beautiful but windy weather — just six minutes after Miller had taken off.

Miller's final leg to Chicago took just two hours. At 7 p.m., he landed at Grant Park on the shore of Lake Mich-igan. The welcoming crowd was so large that the police had to cordon off the landing strip. Miller's mail was un-loaded and rushed to the post office where special mes-sengers delivered it that same night.

Miller had won, but now everyone waited for Gardner's plane. It did not come. Bonfires were lit. Still no Gardner. Finally, a phone call to the nearby Columbia Yacht Club summoned Lipsner. It was Gardner; he and Radel had set down in Westville, Indiana, because of

This cover was flown by Ed Gardner from Chicago to New York as verified by the postmark of September 10, 1918, at 6 a.m., and the New York receiving mark of September 11, 1918, at 7 a.m. Only sixty-eight covers exist that were carried on this flight.

darkness. They would not reach Chicago until the next morning. On the third day, September 7, at 8:17 a.m., Gardner and Radel finally landed safely in Chicago.

On the return flight in the next few days, fate smiled on loser Gardner — in a way. He actually landed in Long Island in the dark, but on the same day he had left Chicago! However, he and Radel were slightly injured when the plane pancaked hard into the ground. Gardner said he got confused, in the dark, with what he thought were 30-foot trees. They turned out to be three-foot bushes.

Probably nowhere are the problems, the daring and hardships of the early airmail pilots so capsulized as they are in the mad, mad, mad race of Max Miller and Ed Gardner. If their flights had shown the possibility of a New York-Chicago route, they had also pointed up the dangers and weaknesses of machines, equipment and safety devices. Not until July 1, 1919 — 11 months later

Ed Gardner (second from left), Max Miller (center) and Eddie Radel (second from right) get ready to fly the mail over Hell Stretch.

— was the route a daily reality. The plane chosen to fly the treacherous route over "Hell Stretch" in regular service is the one pictured on the 24¢ airmail of 1923 (Scott C6) — the DeHavilland DH-4.

The later pilots who flew the reliable DeHavilland had far less trouble than Miller and Gardner. But they did have one big disadvantage: They didn't get to meet half as many people along the way!

Chapter 15

The Unnecessary Issue

Catalogs are perhaps the single most indispensable tool for any collector — including the airmail collector. But, important and useful as they are, they don't tell the full story behind the "whys" and "wherefores" of many stamp issues. The 6¢ United States airmail of 1918 (Scott C1) is a case in point. The catalogs will tell you that this stamp is orange or pale orange in color; that it was issued December 10, 1918, and first used for airmail postage on December 16 of that year; and that it was flat-plate engraved and perforated 11 in sheets of 100. The specialized catalog also will give prices on blocks of four, plate blocks, centerline blocks, blocks of six, arrow blocks and double transfers, as well as on singles, used on cover and first-day covers.

What the catalog doesn't tell you is that this stamp was really an unnecessary issue, printed and dispensed by the Post Office on the supposition that a certain event was going to happen. As such, it might be termed the "least necessary" of all our regular, definitive airmail adhesives.

The story behind the 1918 6¢ stamp really began in August 1918 when Ben Lipsner and others were just beginning to lay plans for extending the airmail service to Chicago. It involves those two pilots, Max Miller and Ed

Gardner, who competed with each other in flying the first New York-Chicago attempt on September 5, 1918. Each pilot had carried about 400 pounds of mail westbound. On the eastbound return flights, Miller flew just 2,974 pieces, while Gardner had but 68 letters and cards.

After these two experimental flights, Otto Praeger reaffirmed that the New York-Chicago airmail route would

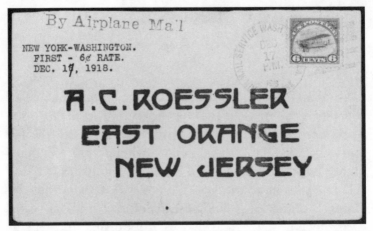

By Airplane Mail

NEW YORK-WASHINGTON.
FIRST - 6¢ RATE.
DEC. 17, 1918.

A.C. ROESSLER
EAST ORANGE
NEW JERSEY

The "unnecessary issue," the 6¢ stamp of 1918, franks this cover to pioneer cachetmaker A.C. Roessler.

be established — but only if it could be guaranteed to be as reliable and efficient as the New York-Washington route had been. Praeger went on to say that the postal rate would be the same on this new route as it was for New York-Washington — that is, 16¢ for the first ounce and 6¢ for each additional ounce.

Praeger's statement was rendered inoperative a short time later when Postmaster General Burleson ordered the rate reduced to 6¢. As mentioned before, this was not really a reduction; the 16¢ airmail stamp of July 1918 included 10¢ for special delivery. All Burleson did was to remove this dime for that special service. He really did not reduce the true air rate.

The Post Office and the Aerial Mail Service were so certain that the new Chicago-New York route would succeed that in Postal Order 2415 of November 30, 1918, the 6¢ rate was made official. The only reason for the 6¢ rate was the proposed new route, and this is why: One pilot noted that airmail letters were trucked to Belmont Park, placed on a swift 90-mile-per-hour airplane, flown to College Park, Maryland, and placed on another truck for Washington. "If the planes flew," he said, "the recipient got his letter almost as fast as if the sender had placed it on the railroad."

The pilot was not merely joking. If you mailed an airmail letter in New York on a Monday afternoon, it would

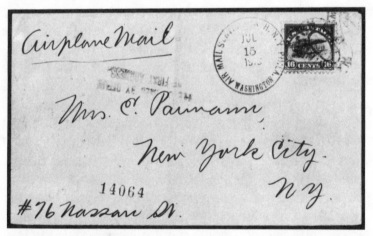

This cover, postmarked July 15, 1918, reflects the rate change from 24¢ to 16¢ for the first ounce.

catch Tuesday's noon flight. It would arrive in Washington at about 3:30 p.m., too late for delivery that day unless it was handled via special delivery. And sometimes, even then, your correspondent would not receive it until Wednesday morning. You could do as well by rail at less postage. Therefore, the special delivery fee included in 16¢ and 24¢ stamps was absolutely necessary with rail service in the New York, Philadelphia, Washington area.

But that special delivery was not necessary for the airmail to beat railway mail between New York and Chicago. The airmail service could do it easily without that extra fee. Thus, the whole reason for the rate reduction from 16¢ to 6¢ was the Chicago-New York route.

The postal patron was not going to be forced to buy a stamp that included special delivery because Burleson no longer needed it to be competitive with rail. If an airmail user used the 6¢ stamp on mail from New York to Washington, he was only kidding himself. Without the special delivery, he was as well-off sending his post by regular first-class mail.

The Post Office itself acknowledged this in a notice issued December 10, 1918, by Third Assistant Postmaster General A.M. Dockery: "Postmasters and other officers and employees of the Postal Service are notified that the department is issuing a new postage stamp of 6¢ denomination. It is intended primarily for the airplane mail service under the new rate effective December 15, 1918, but will be valid for all purposes for which postage stamps of the regular issue are used. The 16¢ aeroplane stamp will still be available for special delivery fee and a single rate of letter postage (six cents) on aeroplane mail. The 24¢ stamp will be available for aeroplane letters weighing in excess of 3 and not more than 4 ounces." Thus the Post Office expected that the 16¢ stamp would still be needed for fast service between New York and Washington.

All of this planning, along with the need for the 6¢ stamp, disappeared December 18, 1918. On that day the first regular scheduled service from New York to Chicago began. It was a disaster. Pilot Leon Smith took off from Belmont Field, Long Island, at 6:15 a.m., but had to return a few moments later when he developed engine trouble. Smith got another plane and took off a second time at

7:20 a.m., bound for Bellefonte, Pennsylvania. He ended up near State College, Pennsylvania, 50 miles from his destination. Engine trouble again. The mail was sent on by train. Two other pilots on separate legs of the westbound mail did not make their destinations. The flights eastbound out of Chicago were also failures.

The Post Office was embarrassed at the poor results on the first day's service. They abandoned the New York-Chicago route, stating that they would try to reopen it sometime in the spring of 1919. With this service between New York and Chicago out, there was now no real need for the 6¢ airmail. That is why I called it an "unnecessary" issue. Before the through service from Manhattan to the Windy City ever became a reality, Burleson had made the ruling that all airmail would go at the 2¢ first-class rate as of July 18, 1919. With that, the useless 6¢ orange airmail of 1918 went down the drain entirely.

Chapter 16

The 2¢ Rate

If you have a regular United States cover postmarked between July 18, 1919, and July 1, 1924, and franked with a first-class 2¢ stamp of that day, the chances are pretty good that what you really have is an airmail cover. Between the first set of United States airmails (Scott C1 to C3) and the second set (C4 to C6), there was a sort of airpost rate vacuum that still causes some confusion for airmail collectors and airmail-rate specialists.

The first 24¢ airmail stamp (Scott C3) was issued May 13, 1918, for use on the new Washington-Philadelphia-New York service that began two days later, on May 15. This stamp, like the next five to follow, also was good for regular post. Therefore, a true first-day cover of the 24¢ airmail is dated May 13 on regular surface mail. It is the "First Trip" cancellation that is dated May 15. The first 24¢ issue also included 10¢ for special delivery service so that the true air rate was 14¢ per ounce. The option to use 14¢ on airmail was not extended, however.

Postmaster General Albert Burleson had the discretionary power in those days to change the rate as he saw fit, and just two months later, he did so. On July 11, the 16¢ airmail stamp was issued. Effective July 15, the airmail rate was lowered to 16¢ for the first ounce and 6¢ for each additional ounce. Again, 10¢ of this stamp went to pay special delivery fees so that the air-rate portion was actually 6¢ — down from 14¢. The sender still had to pay the special delivery cost whether he wanted to or not.

This rate held for five months, until December 15, 1918, when Burleson again changed the airmail stamp to a 6¢ denomination. This stamp (Scott C1) was issued December 10 to coincide with the new Chicago-New York daily airmail service due to start on December 15. The postmaster general really didn't reduce the true air rate to

The 6¢ rate was drawing to a close when this airmail cover was sent by A.C. Roessler on July 16, 1919.

6¢. He merely eliminated the 10¢ special delivery charge from the stamp, leaving it up to the sender to apply the extra postage if he so desired. This option was given the postal patron since the Chicago-New York mail was supposed to arrive in each city in plenty of time to catch the regular scheduled carrier delivery. Ergo, the special delivery was not needed, and the new 6¢ issue reflected this assumption by the Post Office Department. Why the *Scott Postage Stamp Catalogue* lists the first three airmail stamps backwards is anyone's guess. By date of issue or by rate-change progression, they should be displayed from 24¢ to 16¢ to 6¢ (Scott C3 to C2 to C1) on album or exhibit pages.

Airmail rates remained static until July 18, 1919. On that date, according to an official post office domestic airmail rate chart, the rate went to 2¢ per ounce. This rate is annotated in the official chart with this qualification: "Not strictly an airmail rate. Between July 18, 1919, and July 1, 1924, there was no airmail rate and no offer of airmail service. Some mail, however, was carried by plane at the regular first-class rate of 2¢ per ounce."

The United States Post Office Department order, dated July 18, 1919, regarding the implementation of the 2¢ rate. The order is signed by Postmaster General Albert S. Burleson.

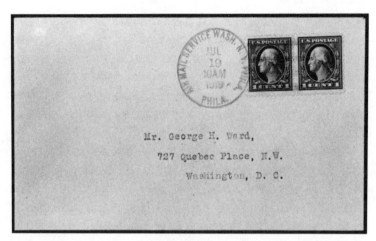

Since July 18 was on a Sunday, this July 19, 1919, cover marks the first day of the 2¢ rate. The rate is covered by two 1¢ stamps.

A 2¢ stamp carried this letter via airmail just one day after airmail rates had been eliminated.

The judgment decision that this was "not really an airmail rate" is borne out by a statement made by Burleson himself. In announcing the 2¢ rate, he said: "The successful operation of the airmail for more than a year and the great development for commerical work on the airplane in that period has taken this phase of mail transportation entirely out of the class of experimental work. The great saving of time now effected over the fastest railroad train between New York and Chicago will enable the department to make a saving in car space of more than twice the cost of the operation of the airmail service on that route. It will, therefore, no longer be necessary to charge more than the regular rate of postage for the transmission of airplane mail."

Though post office documents say that it was not an air rate, this is what Second Assistant Postmaster General Otto Praeger had to say about this new regulation: "The effect of the order is to place all first-class mail on the same basis, and the question of time in mailing will determine whether or not a letter will go by airplane instead of train. Letters in transit which miss train connections will be forwarded by airplane to make up the lost time."

Praeger went on to say that while there was no firm assurance that a letter would go by air, persons could go to postal stations where airmail sacks were assembled and request that their letters be placed in those airmail pouches.

At this point, the first three airmail stamps were abandoned as needed for airpost, and it was no longer necessary to mark letters "Via Air Mail." In Karl Weber's superb history of the government-operated air services, there is an illustration of a cover mailed from the famed airmail collector Harry Truby to George W. Angers. It is cacheted, "First Trip Night Airmail Service San Francisco to Chicago." It is even signed "Jack Knight, U.S. Airmail" as the pilot. The cover has a 2¢ stamp. It is postmarked "August 21, 1923," well within that five-year period when the Post Office maintained that "no airmail service was offered."

What else was going on during this time of "no airmail service?" By using faster planes and dropping the Philadelphia stop, the Washington-New York service was speeded up by 30 minutes. This route was carrying an average of five million letters per year by air. To improve the New York-Chicago route during this time of "no air-mail service," three of the fastest and largest planes available — each with a load capacity of 18,000 letters — were put into use. From New York to Cleveland, eight planes a day were airborne, flying almost 2,000 miles every 24

This 2¢ cover carries a cachet reading, "FIRST TRIP/NIGHT AIR MAIL SERVICE/SAN FRANCISCO TO CHICAGO." The cover is signed by Jack Knight, United States airmail pilot. It is post-marked San Francisco, August 21, 1923. On the back of the cover is a manuscript "Arrived at Chicago/Aug. 23/3 a.m."

hours and carrying something like 85,000 letters daily.

On September 10, 1920, the Omaha-San Francisco route was opened officially. On that same day, the entire

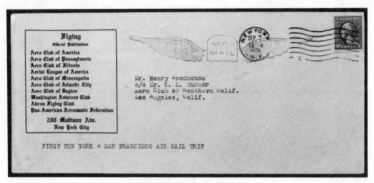

This 2¢ rate cover was carried on the first New York-San Francisco transcontinental airmail flight.

New York-to-San Francisco coast-to-coast mail was placed on a daily basis. In November 1920 the Minneapolis-St. Paul-Chicago leg went into regular service.

In 1921 the Post Office Department paid airplane manufacturers $476,109 for new planes and the remodeling of Army ships for airmail duty. A lot of money was expended for there supposedly being no service. Many other examples could be cited. The United States airmail saw some of its greatest growth during that five-year hiatus of the 2¢ rate when "no airmail service was offered."

Chapter 17

Finding Their Way

Eugene Clay, the renowned "artist of the barnstormers," once painted a picture that shows a pilot leaning out of his low-flying war surplus Jenny and calling down to the engineer of a train running a few feet below his wing tip. "Which way is Springfield?" the pilot is yelling at the locomotive operator.

That well-known painting is not too far a cry from the communications systems that the early airmail pilots had to use to find their way from one end of their airmail runs to the other. In the very early airmail years, the traffic control and weather devices could not even be termed "primitive." They were practically non-existent. The pilots had no way, other than by use of the telephone, to chart their course except by visual landmarks and compasses that were less than accurate. Even these were subject to being shut off at any time by ground fog and magnetic interference.

How a pilot got to the end of his run in 1918 was strictly up to him. One innovative airmail flier, whose route led him over the Allegheny Mountains, decided to combine farmers and phones in what was perhaps the first air traffic and weather report system in airmail history. As the tale goes, this pilot had a farmer friend several miles down the run of his airmail route. He would call the farmer before take-off, asking him how the weather was. The farmer's replies of "fair," "clear," "a little cloudy" and "kinda soupy" left something to be desired in terms

Flying over mountains was hazardous for early pilots who had to rely on primitive methods of traffic control and weather devices.

of accuracy. What was "a little cloudy" to the farmer might be unflyable weather to the pilot.

Many miles from the farmer's house was a tall Allegheny peak. For better weather information, the pilot finally learned to ask the farmer if he could see the peak. These replies of "yes," "no" or "just barely" gave the pilot a closer fix on actual weather conditions. And so a crude form of weather communication was born.

The tools of early air-traffic control were the telephone, perhaps a blackboard and, in more sophisticated airfields, occasionally a table map of sorts covering a wide area. On this crude map, some effort was made to chart the last known position of a particular airmail pilot. Soon the concept of ETA (estimated time of arrival) came along, and some fields began trying to plot the estimated time of arrival of a mail flight. All that really seemed to accomplish, however, was to let the ground personnel know when they should start worrying. There was little they could do in the emergency of an overdue pilot except to report it to Washington.

One of the early pilots, Ken McGregor, writing in the *Saga of the U.S. Air Mail Service,* said, "My altimeter seemed more sensitive to weather conditions than to changes in elevation. It was par for the course to get yourself and Uncle's mail lost once or twice on each trip. The smart pilot would fly low along the railroad tracks until he could read the name on the next station. Some of us knew the railroad better than the conductors on the line."

Map reading was not required of mail pilots in those days for a very simple reason: There were no detailed route maps to give them. McGregor said that three things helped him get from airfield to airfield. One was the "seat of his pants." A second was the ability to recognize every town, river, railroad, farm, courthouse and outhouse along the way. The third, said McGregor, was "a few drops of homing pigeon blood in my veins."

On their weathered, windblown flying jackets, the pilots of that era wore a small insignia reading, "U.S. Aerial Mail Service." This badge served a very useful function in addition to helping the pilots get dates with pretty girls. It gave the pilot legal authority to stop a train and put his mail and himself on board whenever a DH-4 Liberty engine played out and a cornfield landing became necessary. This, said McGregor, was not an infrequent occurrence since there were two or three forced landings or crackups every week in spite of the efforts of mechanics and maintenance men.

In June 1919, an inventor named Willoughby came to

the airmail service with a wonderous gadget. It was supposed to send a radio signal down a cable strung on poles
running from Washington toward Philadelphia. Willoughby carried a receiver that would pick up these signals, thus pointing the plane straight at its destination at
all times. Pilot McGregor was selected to make the first
trial flight with the inventor and his miracle direction
finder. The flier was instructed to stay above the clouds,
out of ground sight, so that the instrument could be given
a thorough testing. The planned test flight from Washington to Philadelphia should have taken about an hour,
even with the slight headwind blowing on that June day.

At about 11:20 a.m., the pair took off and inventor
Willoughby, with the radio-like device on his lap, placed
the earphones on his head. He pointed to the pilot in the
direction his mysterious little box told the plane to go.
One hour went by, and the pilot began to get a little ner-
vous. He wanted to drop down and see the ground, so
long out of sight. He worried that the wind direction had
changed. He wondered if he had some crackpot on board
who was simply trying to sell a wild idea to Uncle Sam.

Finally, about one o'clock, McGregor passed the inventor a note, "Not much gas left — going down." With a gas
gauge near zero and finding unfamiliar territory under his
wings, McGregor set the DH-4 down in a pasture. After
an egg-shell landing, he taxied quickly away from a herd
of cows. He knew cows love to lick the dope used on the
fabric on his wings. On other occasions, they had licked
holes "as big as milk cans" in his lower wings.

A farmer and two children came hurrying over to see
what was going on in the cow pasture. They gawked at the
strange sight of the DH-4. McGregor asked the farmer,
"Where is Philadelphia?" The reply was a curt critique of
inventor Willoughby's new radio direction finder. "I dun-

no," the farmer answered, "but Norfolk, Virginia, is right over there."

Willoughby was crestfallen. His dreams of a gigantic contract with the new Aerial Mail Service had gone up — not in smoke — but in the loud and erratic static noises he thought were directional signals. He was 90 miles from Philly and 180 degrees in the wrong direction.

That first trial of a device to guide a mail plane flying out of sight of ground reference has a familiar ring. It was just a little more than a year prior to this that George Boyle had flown the first airmail out of Washington and in this same wrong direction. Boyle ended up crashing in Waldorf, Maryland, and was drummed out of the service. Like the name of George Boyle, that of Willoughby also disappears from the rest of the airmail story.

By 1920, however, the entire airmail system was linked by radio. This included airfields, the Post Office Department in Washington and all the repair depots. The radio used signals and Morse code — not voice. Despite that shortcoming, the Army, Navy and Aerial Mail Service had established a communications system independent from the phone lines leased by other government agencies. It was cheaper than the telephones and provided the government with a backup network, should it ever be needed. Over that new network went messages, orders to dispatch planes, weather reports, emergency bulletins and all types of routine communications. The radio network was working well, but leaders of the airmail service, such as Otto Praeger and Ben Lipsner, considered it only a stepping stone.

Chapter 18

Coast to Coast

The important events by date that led up to the coast-to-coast airmail attempt are as follows:

May 15, 1918 — First scheduled airmail service New York-Philadelphia-Washington. Army pilots fly the mail. Postal rate is 24¢ per ounce (Scott C3), including special delivery charges.

July 15, 1918 — Airmail rate reduced to 16¢ per ounce (Scott C2); rate still provides for special delivery.

August 12, 1918 — United States Post Office Department takes over the mail. Civilian pilots now flying; the Army is out after 87 days.

September 5-10, 1918 — Gardner and Miller fly experimental flights from New York to Chicago and return. No regular service begun.

December 10, 1918 — Airmail rate reduced to 6¢ per ounce (Scott C1); no special delivery provided.

May 15, 1919 — Chicago-to-Cleveland service inaugurated.

July 1, 1919 — New York-to-Chicago regular service established.

May 15, 1920 — New York-to-Chicago route extended westward to Omaha, via Iowa City, Iowa.

This now brings us to the beginning of coast-to-coast

flights — in daylight only. On September 20, 1920, the Post Office Department started regular service on the final leg of its transcontinental dream — from Omaha to San Francisco. Great improvements in the Liberty engine that powered the DeHavilland DH-4 had made this westward extension feasible.

The first plane to the far west flew via Omaha and North Platte, Nebraska; Cheyenne, Rawlins and Rock Springs, Wyoming; Salt Lake City, Utah; Elko and Reno, Nevada; and on into San Francisco. The first flight averaged 80 miles per hour and was flown without a single forced landing. Neither weather nor equipment failure plagued this flight as it had the Gardner-Miller attempts just two years previously.

This initial flight carried 16,000 letters and arrived in San Francisco 22 hours ahead of the best possible time by railway mail — assuming the trains had made all proper connections on time. A few months later (May 31, 1921) — partly as an economic measure — all other airmail routes were discontinued, leaving the New York-Chicago-Omaha-San Francisco schedule as the only airmail route approved and funded by Congress.

Though the 22-hour saving over train mail was increasing the public use of airmail, the time saving was severely restricted by the daylight-only flying practice. If the route could be maintained on a through-service basis — day and night — the actual delivery time saved could be doubled. The Post Office Department decided to go for broke on at least one day-and-night attempt. On February 22, 1921, two planes left New York and two left San Francisco. They were to fly coast-to-coast both day and night and in the middle of some severe winter weather. Three of the four flight attempts met with failure.

In an ironic twist to the performance record of the DeHavilland aircraft, one of the New York pilots was forced down shortly after take-off. The other plane from New York made it to Chicago, but was stalled there by bad weather. The first San Francisco plane crashed in Nevada, killing its pilot. The second San Francisco plane, flown by pilot Nutter, left at 4:30 a.m. and made it to Reno where pilot Eaton took the ship. A pilot named Murray replaced Eaton — probably at Salt Lake City — and flew to Cheyenne, arriving at about 5 p.m., just 12 hours after Nutter had left the west coast.

As the next pilot, Frank Yager, left Cheyenne, the quick darkness of a winter evening was closing in. Yager landed

This cover is believed to have been carried on Jack Knight's famous February 1921 night flight.

in the dark at North Platte, Nebraska, just a little before 8 p.m. At least one out of four through-flight tries was still a success after 15 straight hours in the air.

It was at North Platte, that cold, dark winter night, that Jack Knight began the flight that was to make him an airmail — and a flying — immortal. Knight was delayed two to three hours from his regular take-off time by a broken tail skid. It was nearly 11 p.m. when his DeHavilland got away from North Platte and into complete blackness and a rather low ceiling, reported at 2,000 feet. Knight said later that as he flew over small towns, such as Lexington and Kearney, he saw the fires the Nebraskans had lit to guide his way.

At 1:15 on the morning of February 23, Knight landed

Flying from North Platte, Nebraska, to Chicago, through fog, snow and sleet, pilot Jack Knight saved the airmail service from political hatchetmen.

at Omaha — his 276-mile leg of the mission apparently finished. He was tired and ready to turn the mail over to a new pilot and plane due in for the last leg to Chicago. But fate said otherwise. His replacement had been grounded in Chicago. There was no one to fly the next jump — except Knight himself and his same DeHavilland.

He agreed to keep going, although ahead of him

loomed one of the longest hops of the entire schedule, 435 more miles into Chicago. Knight was completely unfamiliar with the Omaha-Chicago route, and as if that were not enough, snow was predicted. He found the snow at Des Moines. It was so bad he could not attempt his scheduled landing for gasoline. He flew on to the next field, Iowa City, Iowa. The regular crew had gone home, and only the watchman was there to help guide him in. It is reported he had 10 minutes worth of fuel left when he set his ship down at Iowa City. As he and the watchmen fueled his plane, it began to sleet.

How he did it over a strange course, in the fog and sleet, and exhausted, no one can say. But at 8:40 a.m., Knight landed the mail at Checkerboard Field in Maywood, just outside Chicago. Knowledgeable flying experts termed it the greatest single example of dead-reckoning and that seat-of-the-pants flying technique ever seen.

The rest was anticlimax. Other pilots took the mail from Chicago into New York. Thanks to pilot Knight, the mail from San Francisco arrived in New York at 4:50 p.m., February 23 — 33 hours and 21 minutes after it had left San Francisco. Knight's legendary flight was made more than three years ahead of the time the Post Office Department was ready to institute regular night-flying service coast to coast.

Yet to come were the safety measures of two-way radios, radio-equipped airfields and that "lighted highway" so necessary to flying in the dark. Not until July 1, 1924, was Knight's flight repeated.

The 8¢ issue of 1923 (Scott C4) was the first stamp intended for airmail that did not picture a plane. It showed, instead, a wooden propeller. The 16¢ of 1923 (Scott C5) exhibits the airmail insignia worn by the early pilots. The 24¢ (Scott 6) reverted to planes and shows the

**The United States Post Office issued three new airmail stamps —
6¢, 8¢ and 24¢ — in August 1923 for the new night-flying airmail
service between New York and San Francisco.**

sturdy DeHavilland. Meanwhile, the rates moved to 8¢
per ounce in each of the three zones. These three 1923
airmail issues were printed primarily for the night-flying
service. Thus, Jack Knight and his fellow "night-flyers"
prompted — among other things — the creation of a new
set of airmail stamps.

Chapter 19

Front Office Quartet

When Otto Praeger, the "first airmail enthusiast," left the key aerial post of second assistant postmaster general in 1921, he was replaced by Colonel E.H. Shaughnessy. Postmaster General Burleson also was superceded at the same time by Will Hays. Both Colonel Shaughnessy and Hays came in under the new Harding administration. Hays was later to become the czar of the motion picture industry, and he is undoubtedly better known for that role than as a postmaster general.

The first important airmail actions of the Hays-Shaughnessy team were to eliminate the original New York-to-Washington airmail route and to cancel two feeder routes hooking up with the transcontinental mail. The New York-Washington service was canceled as of June 1, 1921. The official reason given was that the service no longer had any particular usefulness. It had been kept open, said Shaughnessy, in the hope that it ultimately would become an operating segment of a longer route running from major New England cities to southeastern metropolitan centers.

When the congressional monies were not forthcoming, the Post Office Department shut down the original airmail route, saying that funds spent there could be better used on the more important transcontinental Columbia route from New York to San Francisco. Thirty days later, on July 1, 1921, Shaughnessy also closed the two feeder routes running from Chicago to St. Louis and from Chicago to the Twin Cities. At this point, the only government airmail route in the United States was the transcontinental Columbia route.

The fields at Newark, Bustleton, College Park, St. Louis, Minneapolis and LaCrosse were abandoned. All refueling stops serving these routes also were shut down. Personnel and equipment were transferred to the transcontinental so far as was possible. To John Q. Public, all of this looked as though the airmail was being gradually phased

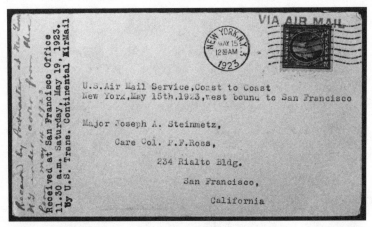

Carried coast to coast, this cover bears a typewritten receiving inscription, "Received at San Francisco Office, 11:30 a.m. Saturday May 19, 1923. By U.S. Trans. Continental Airmail." Only three covers are known to exist.

out of existence. To counter that attitude, the Hays-Shaughnessy regime issued the following statement: "This action is in no way to be construed as a lessening of interest in nor a curtailment of airmail development."

Standardization and cost economizing seemed to be the new watchword. Several different operating divisions were reduced to just three: the Eastern Division (New York-Chicago); the Central Division (Chicago-Rock Springs) and the Western (Rock Springs-San Francisco). Employee staffs were cut from 521 to 382; of this last number, only 39 were pilots. The many varieties of planes being used were cut to just one — an improved version of the single-engined DH-4 that had served the airmail since its beginning. The ready availability of many of these ships had more to do with their selection than their airmail hauling capabilties.

What seemed like rash and harsh actions by Shaughnessy proved in retrospect to have been needed steps to get the service in better and trimmer shape for its coast-to-coast flying.

While still in office, and just before he died, Shaughnessy set down his ideas on the future of the airmail. In essence, he stated that he hoped that private commercial aviation would soon take over the airmail. "The Department," said Shaughnessy, "does not feel that it should operate an airmail service any more than it should operate a steamboat or railway service."

Shaughnessy was succeeded by another non-pilot, Colonel Paul Henderson, a former Army ordnance officer. He inherited a weather service comprising 17 stations along the transcontinental route and a Shaughnessy edict that had banned all night flying until effective lighting could be installed. It was this route-lighting problem that Henderson turned his energies to first. By 1923, he had the Chicago-Cheyenne leg ready for a night-flight test trip. The terminal fields had boundary and flood lights plus tower beacons in excess of 500 million candlepower. Emergency fields every 25 miles, with lesser lighting, also were made ready. The new modified planes were fitted with landing lights and parachute flares to find a set-down spot if no field was nearby.

In August 1923, four days of test flights were flown with no accidents or apparent problems. Henderson was something of a perfectionist, however, and it wasn't until July 1, 1924, that day/night flying began on the transcon-

This cover was carried on the first night airmail flight from San Francisco to Chicago. It is postmarked August 21, 1923.

tinental. By this time, Henderson had extended the "Highway of Lights" to Rock Springs, Wyoming. The Air Mail Service won the Collier Trophy in 1923 and 1924 for the "greatest achievement in aviation in America."

Paul Henderson might even be said to have had a hand in the Ford Trimotor. He suggested to Bill Stout that his first single-engine, all-metal plane could be made even better and safer if Stout would make it a little larger and add a couple engines.

The fourth and last member of the front-office quartet who built the airmail is W. Irving Glover. He, too, was a non-flier. Glover's major accomplishment was the successful implementing of the day/night transcontinental mail that Shaughnessy and Henderson had begun. It was Glover who also was postally responsible for the covers that exist from the cross-country flights of the dirigible

Second Assistant Postmaster General Irving Glover studies a banner proposed for all airmail fields. Glover guided the successful beginning of the day-and-night transcontinental airmail.

Shenandoah made during 1924. He gave official postal approval for those carries when others had denied it.

Collectors won't find their names in any encyclopedia that I know of, but Otto Praeger, E.H. Shaughnessy, Paul Henderson and Irving Glover were indeed among the trailblazers of the American airmail. For four non-pilots, they flew the front office in those critical early years as well as the pioneer airmen flew their DeHavillands.

Chapter 20

Highway of Lights

When Ed Gardner and Max Miller completed their September 5, 1918, first flights from New York to Chicago, the field they landed on in the Windy City was a park bordering Lake Michigan. The crowd gathered at that park had started several bonfires when darkness came to help light the way for the pilots at night. Thus was born, somewhat spontaneously, the first "lighted airfield."

A series of test flights August 21-24, 1923, were the first to involve night flying from Chicago to Cheyenne over the new lighted airways. This cover is postmarked Cheyenne, Wyoming, August 21, with a New York receiving mark of August 22.

The airmail moved west and, ultimately, on September 8, 1920, reached San Francisco. The pilots were restricted to flying in daylight hours only, however, and the airmail rested after dark. Planes averaged about 80 miles per hour in covering the three legs of the flight: New York to Chicago, Chicago to Omaha, and Omaha to San Francisco.

Though the daylight flying improved postal service by 22 hours over the best possible time a train could make, it

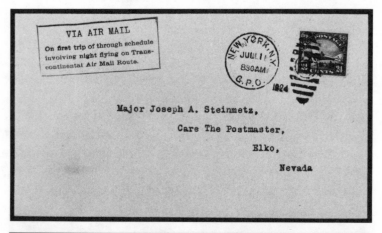

The transcontinental airmail route involving night flying was officially opened July 1, 1924. This flight cover is postmarked New York, New York, July 1, and backstamped Elko, Nevada, July 2.

was apparent that the real time advantages of airmail versus trains would never be realized until planes did what trains were doing — traveled by night. During spring and summer of 1923, work was begun on a lighted airway between Cheyenne, Wyoming, and Chicago. The pilots needed geographic landmarks, which, in the daytime, they had in abundance. This first lighted airway was to be their ground reference benchmark by night.

The segment from Cheyenne to Chicago was chosen for night flying for two reasons. First, it was the middle of the three segments and would allow daylight flight on each side of the portion. More important, the pilots would be flying largely over the Midwestern plains area — the safest ground for night flying in case of emergency landings.

A pace of 33 to 36 hours from San Francisco to New York seemed possible by taking off from San Francisco in the early morning, flying by daylight to Cheyenne, flying by night from Cheyenne to Chicago, and from Chicago to New York on the second day. The heart of this entire plan of coast-to-coast continuous flying appears on the 5¢ carmine and blue airmail issue of 1928. The vignette shows an airmail station with a mail plane in the background. These stations were really emergency landing fields, and 34 of them were set up between Chicago and Cheyenne — one about every 25 to 30 miles.

Their construction and layout were almost identical. Each had roughly 40 acres as a landing field, bordered with landing lights. Each also had a 50-foot tower with a continuously rotating beacon, a shed to house either electric battery power or a gas generator, and a telephone. A caretaker kept each station operational. Stamp collectors can identify all but the phone and caretaker on the 5¢ airmail stamp of 1928 (Scott C11). In between these stations, approximately every three miles, a flashing gas beacon was installed. There were 289 of these flasher units —

This beacon and 40-acre landing field at Sherman Hill, Wyoming,
is the airmail station pictured on the United States 1928 5¢ airmail
stamp. With 34 such stations between Chicago and Cheyenne —
interlaced with 289 flashing gas beacon lights — the night-flying
pilots literally flew a highway of lights.

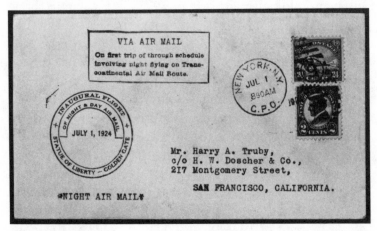

The four-line cachet on this first-flight cover reads, "VIA AIR
MAIL/On first trip of through schedule/involving night flying on
Trans-/continental Air Mail Route."

flashing once every second — between Chicago and Cheyenne. They were powered by cylinders of acetylene gas.

Five terminal landing fields also were established along this route. Their makeup was much like the 34 stations, except for a much more powerful beacon. These five fields possessed 500,000-candlepower lights that were visible from the air for 150 miles in clear weather. Station beacons were smaller in size (18 inches versus 36 inches) and of just 50,000 candlepower, visible ideally for about 60 to 70 miles.

Once the "highway of light" was complete, it was necessary to equip the night-flying aircraft with running lights, landing lights and two parachute flares that could light up an area about one mile in diameter should the pilot have to set down in an emergency. Seventeen planes were so outfitted and used only on the night-flying leg of the schedule.

By August 1923, the lighted airway was ready, and the first regularly scheduled night flights were flown as a test of the coast-to-coast airmail. However, this was only a test, and it lasted just four days. Regular and permanent service did not begin until July 1, 1924.

The lighted airways proved so effective, and the safety record so good for the night pilots, that the flyway was extended eastward from Chicago to New York in the spring of 1925. In the fall of that year, the lighted flyway was lengthened westward from Cheyenne to Salt Lake City. The flyway cost about $540,000 and extended for 2,045 miles. A pilot could fly day or night from Salt Lake City to New York and be in touch with ground reference points all the way.

To help finance the flyway, the airmail postal rates were not only increased but also were exactly dove-tailed into the same three segments that the planes flew on transcontinental flights. If you lived in New York City, the rate was 8¢ per ounce within the New York-Chicago zone. If your letter went west of Chicago but east of Cheyenne, this rate was 16¢ per ounce; west of Cheyenne was zone three and 24¢ per ounce. To handle this new rate-zone system, the three airmail issues of 1923 were needed. The public was confused by the segmented-zone plan, and many felt that the lack of use of airmail in general was certainly not helped by this complex rate policy.

From that airfield in the middle of a racetrack, the airmail service had come to a highway of lights extending two-thirds of the way across the country. The airmail service had accomplished its coast-to-coast nighttime flying objective in just seven short years.

Chapter 21

The Early Pilots

The time: early 1920s. The place: Cleveland, Ohio, a rooming house on 118th Street near St. Clair Avenue. The cast: Frank Click (a youngster, age seven or so), his mother, Laura, and a dozen or more early airmail pilots. With the help of some sprightly reminiscing by Frank Click, a stamp collector who lived in Daytona Beach, Florida, we go back in time to live for a few moments with a young lad and some of his best buddies — the early airmail fliers.

The beginning of Click's story goes back to a day when his mother, who had recently divorced, was returning from New York via train. She made the acquaintance of a young airmail pilot, Jack Davis. "That broke the ice," Click recalled, "and from then on at least five airmail pilots rented rooms in our house at any given time." Some of the fliers that Click remembered, in addition to Davis, are Wesley L. Smith, Elmer Van Atta, Ernest Allison, Charles Hayden Ames, J.T. Christensen, Elmer Leonhardt, Paul (Dog) Collins and various others whose names Click could not specifically recall. His mother later became engaged to Elmer Van Atta, but before they could marry, he was killed in a crash at Mineola, New York. In the early 1920s, Van Atta had flown the New York-Washington run out of Potomac Park and later the New York-Cleveland leg.

Elmer Leonhardt was known around the rooming house as the "Lucky Dollar" pilot. During one of his airmail flights, some wiring in the cockpit area shorted out. Leonhardt took a dollar bill from his pocket, wrapped it as insulation around the hot wire and continued on to land safely at his destination. From then on, he was known as the "Lucky Dollar" pilot. True to the traditional pilots' penchant for superstition, Leonhardt kept that same dollar bill at hand in the cockpit of every plane he flew subsequently. Leonhardt was based in Cleveland in those days, flying the Cleveland-New York segment. His major distinction in airmail history is that he flew the first eastbound Chicago-Cleveland portion of the first transcontinental daylight attempt on September 10, 1920.

Frank Click remembered: "There were a few times I can recall when a pilot flying in from New York would circle our house at a low altitude. He would holler down for someone to come out to the airport and pick him up. Somebody at the house had a Templer automobile that was the usual airport taxi."

On one occasion when a pilot was circling the house, he dropped a bundle from the plane. The bundle landed in the Click front yard. It was addressed to another pilot living at the house. A note enclosed said that the bundle contained some dirty clothes that the addressee had left at his lodgings in New York. The note went on to say that the New York landlady could no longer stand the package's fragrance and had given it to the pilot. The pilot said that he couldn't stand it either and was getting rid of the clothes via "air-drop."

Some of the Cleveland fliers were "bumped off." That was their own expression, Click recalled, for being killed in a crash. They felt that the ground came up and "bumped" them. Most of all, the fliers feared the mountains in Pennsylvania on the Cleveland-New York jump. According to historical sources, J.T. Christensen was killed on a Chicago-Omaha mail run, but Click remembered him also hitting the high-level bridge in Cleveland during a fog and sustaining injuries.

Another pilot, Wesley Smith, had an unusual facial feature — one side was much darker than the other. Fire

Pilot Wesley Smith, one of the first to fly the transcontinental route, was a roomer at the Click boarding house.

broke out in his plane on an airmail trip, and Smith, to keep the flames away from the gas tank, flew at a tilt until he could land. Flying this way, according to Click, the fire licked at Smith's face slightly, causing the permanent disfiguring. Smith escaped from his plane on landing, shortly before the fire consumed it completely.

Wesley Smith's claims to fame as an early airmail flier involved flying the westbound New York-Cleveland leg on the July 1, 1924, first day of regular service of the day

and night transcontinental airmail and making the re-
verse trip — Cleveland to New York — on the July 2
eastbound journey.

Click recalled that it was the pilots who taught him to
tell time. They frequently took him along on their many
trips out for chop suey, their favorite dish. They were a
great and lively bunch of young men, Click said, and they
were forever playing pranks on one another. One repeated

**This cover was carried on the first scheduled flight involving
night flying on the transcontinental route. Pilot Wesley Smith
flew the westbound New York-Cleveland leg on July 1, 1924.**

prank, played at one time or another by most of them, was the slat removal gag. For this, the wooden bed slats were taken out, and twine was tied across the bed frame to support the mattress. The next pilot in that bed (they rotated bunks as flights came in and out) would soon end up on the floor. As a seven-year-old, Click's reward for helping tie the twine and keeping his mouth shut was a regular payoff of 25¢.

One pilot — Click couldn't remember which one — offered him a chance to fly with him to New York on a regular airmail run. This, of course, was impossible and against a few dozen government regulations. When the promised day arrived, the weather was bad, cold and snowing, thus offering the pilot his "out" for not taking young Frank along.

On another occasion, a brand new airplane was delivered to the Cleveland field for one of the pilots. He was to go to the airport and take it up on a pre-flight checkout trip. For three days before the plane's arrival, the pilot had bragged about "his" new plane to his fellow fliers. Click accompanied the pilot and two others to the field for the test flight. It was a beautiful ship — dark and shiny, he recalled. On take-off, one of the wheels hit a chuckhole and came off, causing the plane to careen off the runway and damage a wing tip. The test pilot was subjected to a royal roasting. His experience, the current status of his license, whether he had ever soloed, his flight training and even his family lineage were good naturedly called to question by the two observing pilots.

Ernest Allison was one of the boarding house birdmen best remembered by Click. Allison was flying out of New York's Hazelhurst Airfield in those days on the New York-Cleveland hop. He was later to fly the Cleveland-New York final eastbound leg on that same February 22-23, 1921, coast-to-coast day-and-night first attempt that brought Jack Knight to flying immortality. Click wished that he could remember the antics of the boarding house gang more clearly and in greater detail. "I didn't realize," he said, "that I was living in the middle of some history in the making. I do recall one thing, though. The pilots always called their airplane 'airships,' and I could never figure out why since they didn't have any sails."

Frank Click learned to fly in 1937. "But I never had the spirit for it that those young men in Cleveland had," he said. Twelve similar young men with "spirit" lost their lives in a one-year span flying that "Hell Stretch" run over the Alleghenies between Cleveland and New York. Thanks to Frank Click, we have had a brief glimpse into the lives of that Cleveland boarding house gang of the early '20s. They, too, were some of those "young men with spirit" who made the airmail work.

Chapter 22

World's Flyingest Man

E. Hamilton Lee recalled clearly the trials, the humor and the experiences of his early days as one of the airmail's premier pilots. Back in 1918 his fellow pilots, mechanics and airfield managers called him "Ham," but few could ever learn from him what the "E" stood for. Early in his airmail flying career he had another nickname: "the one-hundred percent pilot." If Ham Lee took off for a destination, he always seemed to make it one way or another. Never mind what other pilots had done before him or whether there was any flying on that day — Ham Lee always got through.

Ham Lee stayed a one-hundred percenter until one bleak day near Newark, New Jersey, when he was flying through rain and fog and perhaps pushing that percentage too hard. Occasionally, he could see the ground below him, but nothing was visible in the soupy weather ahead of his clunker plane. Suddenly, he crashed into and straight through a tree and hit the ground hard. He found himself surrounded by a wrecked airplane, but he was only slightly bruised.

As he walked away, somewhat gimpily, he decided then and there to start following that famous old fliers' maxim that goes like this: "There are old pilots and there are

111

bold pilots, but there are no old bold pilots." He said it was on that day that he determined to become the best and the oldest pilot in the airmail service and to heck with being a "one-hundred percenter."

Ham Lee reached that goal. He began flying the airmail in December 1918. In the spring of 1919, he was appointed senior No. 1 airmail pilot, a post he held for another 30 years until his "retirement" on July 1, 1949. He "retired" into a pilot's job with United Airlines, flying a DC-

Senior airmail pilot E. Hamilton "Ham" Lee in his official mail pilot's uniform. He flew the mail for nine years.

3 Mainliner from San Francisco to Los Angeles. Ham Lee accumulated a record 4.4 million air miles in 27,812 flying hours during his airmail and airline careers that bracketed 36 years. On his final retirement, he was the world's "flyingest" man.

His proudest recollection was that in that span of 36 years, he never lost a piece of airmail or injured a passenger. That 27,812 hours of flight time translates into three years, two months and four days that Ham Lee actually spent in the clouds flying Jennies, DeHavillands, Standards, Douglases and other types of planes.

Lee attributed his long flying career to staying in good enough shape to pass the pilots' required annual physicals. That routine for him included "eating all that I wanted, never taking any physical exercise and smoking nothing except the finest cigars, one after another all day long." Some of Ham's co-pilots complained that his cigar fumes so polluted the cockpit area that the pilots were flying on instruments even on clear days.

How did this most durable of all the early airmail pilots react to the job of flying the United States mail in planes

This cover commemorates the golden anniversary flight of old DeHavilland No. 249 from coast to coast 50 years after its first trip in 1918. The cover is signed at the upper left by Bill Hackbarth, who flew the restored airplane, and by Ham Lee.

that were often less than airworthy? For one thing, Ham said he hated to be "overflown." In those beginning days, it was considered humiliating for one pilot to sit on the ground because of weather and have another "overfly" him. It was, however, a rare pilot who overflew Ham Lee. Most who tried it more than once either crashed, quit flying altogether or gave up being a "hundred percenter." Lee said he tried to make a study of his fellow pilots' crashes to avoid whatever caused them. "I figured I could whip any condition this way, and I believe I did," he proclaimed.

He also took a cynical view of the gadgetry that came into airmail cockpits in the 1920s. All of the new gauges and radio beams did not deter his passion for knowing every prominent landmark along his route. If the gadgets disagreed with the landmarks, Lee followed what he saw on the ground, not what he heard and saw in the cockpit. "A beep in the ears is no substitute for the brains in between," he opined.

The senior No. 1 pilot did not like night flying either, at least not until he learned that his mileage pay was going to be doubled for flying after dark. He finally learned to fly more relaxed at night than in the daytime, a trait that many pilots develop. Lee's true reason for not liking night flying was blunt and honest. "Flying," he said, "is work. Who wants to work nights?" He did not go in for some of the hot-dog manuevers of some early airmail fliers. Close to the ground, he did everything by the book. There were no "Split-S" landings for Ham Lee — just straight in and by the numbers. He reserved any stunting — and he did a lot of it — for times when he was at least 5,000 feet high.

He hated — as did most pilots — the open cockpits of the early aircraft. They could literally freeze a pilot on some of the 20-below-zero flights that Ham Lee made over Iowa and Nebraska in the winter seasons. He would pad his fur flying suit with newspapers and even tape a piece of fur across his nose. Still, he shivered and shook as much as his airplanes.

His penchant for knowing the landmarks instead of relying on instruments alone is illustrated by a story he told of another airmail pilot. It seems this pilot's magnetic compass was deflected 100 degrees or more by some engine parts he was carrying in the mail cockpit. This flier had left New York for Cleveland on a hazy, murky evening. When he started to land, he was over the Atlantic Ocean. Thinking it must be Lake Erie, he turned left and found New England, which he promptly decided must be Ohio. Still searching for Cleveland, he ran out of gas and cracked up. He pounded on a farmhouse door in Connecticut and asked of the old Yankee who opened it, "Where's Cleveland." "Cleveland's dead," said the farmer. "Hoover's president now."

Chapter 23

The Strike

When Ham Lee decided to give up any thoughts of the banking business and go in for flying, he made his way to the Pallisard Aviation School in Chicago. Though lessons were $75 an hour, it was less than a first-rate choice. Pallisard's total assets included five students, two combination mechanic-pilots and one decrepit airplane that was out of commission most of the time. It took Ham Lee one and half years to finally get in just four and a half hours of actual flying time. He soloed, at last, in 1916.

When World War I began, he talked himself into an army pilot instructor's job at Chanute Field in Rantoul, Illinois. Along with many other Army-affiliated fliers, he went to work for Otto Praeger and the new airmail outfit in late 1918. At that time, Ham recalled, airmail letters were trucked to Belmont Park, Long Island, placed on a "swift" 90-mile-per-hour airplane, flown to College Park, Maryland, and then trucked into Washington. "If the planes flew," said Lee, "the recipient got his letter almost as fast as if the sender had placed it on the Pennsy."

Ham Lee became involved with a pilot named Leon Smith in one of aviation's classic confrontations with safety practices. It led to one of today's important air safety rules. Early pilots of that time were taking far too many risks, and too many of them were being killed. Yet, it seemed that every time a flight was scrubbed because of weather, Congress threatened to cancel appropriations for the "impractical" new mail system. The Post Office Department finally issued a firm order: "Fly by compass, regardless of weather. Visibility is not necessary." Pilots who thought the weather too risky for a take-off began to develop all sorts of "engine trouble." When the fog hung low and it was ceiling zero, it seemed that every plane had "engine trouble."

Pilot Leon Smith was the first to refuse to directly obey the Post Office edict during one soupy day at Belmont. The airfield manager cabled Washington, and the answer came back that Pilot Smith was to take off promptly and without further delay. Smith refused a second time, and Ham Lee was called in to take his flight. Lee told the manager he wouldn't go either. "If the weather is too bad for Smith, it's too bad for me. His judgment is as good as mine," said Ham Lee. Smith and Lee were both ordered dismissed from the airmail service.

Almost at once all airmail pilots struck in sympathy with Smith and Lee. For about 36 hours, no airmail moved anywhere. Lee and a delegation went to Otto Praeger, who negotiated the pilot complaints with political higher-ups. The pilots won. From that day on, no pilot ever had to take off because an airfield manager said so. The new rule had a unique twist: If the manager thought that the weather was fit for flying, he had to show the pilots that it was by flying himself. Even today, that rule still stands. The modern airline captain is the supreme judge on flying conditions. It is he who says "we go" or "we don't go," and no member of airline management can overrule him.

Lee was assigned to the New York-Washington run from December 28, 1918, to August 1, 1920. On at least half of his flights, he flew the specially built Standard JR-1B mail planes. There were only six of these ships ever used, and Ham Lee had the dubious honor of demolishing one-third of the Standard fleet. The first Standard he cracked up was near Newark. He lost his second one in the northern Mississippi valley during the winter of 1921.

Like other pilots, Lee rated the Standard as a good low-altitude ship, alert and responsive but sluggish on take-off and with a tendency to overheat. The Standards were withdrawn from the New York-Washington run and sent west to fly the new St. Louis-Chicago and Chicago-Minneapolis routes.

Ironically, Ham Lee was transferred with the Standards. On August 16, 1920, he was the first to fly the south-

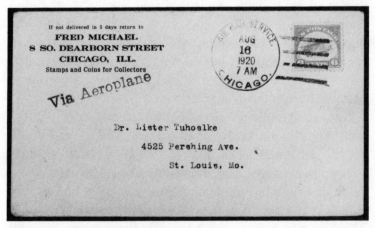

This cover was carried on the Chicago-St. Louis leg of the experimental St. Louis-Chicago and return route on August 16, 1920.

bound route on the new Chicago-St. Louis feeder line. On November 29, 1920, he flew another first — the first flight on the permanent Chicago-Twin Cities service. But this time he got away from the Standard, using a twin-DeHavilland for the first trip.

Lee was later based in Omaha where for 10 years he

carried the mail on the Omaha-Chicago leg. He flew for an additional seven years on the Omaha-Cheyenne route. In 1924 Ham Lee was summoned back east on a special assignment. On July 1 of that year he flew one of two aircraft on the New York-Cleveland hop of the first day-night regular transcontinental service. During those years, fighting the cold and winds between Chicago, Omaha and Cheyenne, Ham Lee often got to participate in the cold weather midwestern start-up rituals for an airplane en-

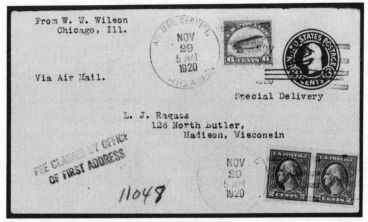

Experimental flights were made November 29, 1920, between Chicago and Minneapolis with stops at Madison, and LaCrosse, Wisconsin, and St. Paul, Minnesota.

gine. In those early morning hours, it was often necessary to pour 16 gallons of boiling water into a DeHavilland's radiator and follow that with 12 gallons of heated motor oil to even have a prayer of turning the engine over. And, if that engine didn't start quickly after just a few tugs at the propeller, the water and oil had to be completely drained before they froze. Then, the whole icy routine had to be done again.

When Ham Lee finally made it to that cushy, enclosed cockpit of the DC-3 Mainliner, he made it a rule never to leave his pilot's seat to mix with the passengers. Resolute and cautious, he felt that two pilots were hired to make flying safer, not to have one play the public relations

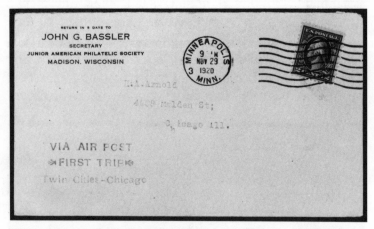

This cover was carried on the first return flight on the Twin Cities-Chicago route on November 29, 1920.

game with the passengers. "If they want to know how wide the wings are, the stewardess can tell 'em," was the way he put it.

Ham Lee was something else besides the premier airmail pilot of the early days and the senior No. 1 airmail pilot for 30 years. He was also a kind and gracious gentleman who took the time and effort to respond to all the questions of an airmail history nut who wanted to know everything about what really went on in those open-cockpit, glory days of the American airmail. For his help and his cooperation in spinning this tale, my deep respects and sincere thanks to Captain E. Hamilton Lee. He was the exception to that old fliers maxim. He was one of the old, bold pilots.

Chapter 24

Hell Stretch

On March 5, 1925, Second Assistant Postmaster General Paul Henderson went to a luncheon sponsored by the New York State Chamber of Commerce in New York City. In his post-luncheon speech, Henderson revealed publicly that the Post Office Department would begin the long-sought New York-to-Chicago overnight airmail service "by June 1 or sooner." Henderson went on to say that with ten million people within "striking distance" of New York City and that with about half that number in or near Chicago, the new service should attract enough mail volume to justify its existence.

The plan, he said, was to have a plane leave each city at 9:30 p.m., arriving at the other destination by 5:30 in the morning, in plenty of time to catch the first mail deliveries in those two largest cities. Henderson's tentative schedule called for three stops: Bellefonte, Pennsylvania, and Cleveland and Bryan, Ohio. Planes would be changed at Cleveland, with the other two stops used for refueling.

The announcement must have engendered favorable response from those chamber of commerce business leaders. For many months, shippers, bankers and other businessmen had been clamoring for a New York-to-Chicago overnight airmail. Many had found that the 32-hour coast-to-coast day/night airmail was a great business boon and had petitioned the Post Office Department for quicker deliveries between Manhattan and the center of midwestern commerce.

Long before Henderson's speech, the Post Office De-

This cover was carried on the first overnight flight from New York to Chicago. It is postmarked Bellefonte, Pennsylvania.

partment already had conducted a survey in both cities. The results showed that thousands would use such service. The then-current daytime schedule had the airmail leaving New York at 10 a.m. and Chicago at 7:30 a.m.

Carl F. Egge, general superintendent of the United States airmail from 1921 to 1926.

Both of these departures made delivery impossible until the following day.

Henderson also had commissioned Carl Egge, general superintendent of airmail service, to evaluate the practicality of flying at night over the "Hell Stretch" of the Allegheny Mountains. Egge's numerous trips over the terrain — both on the ground and in the air — had led him to believe that a night-flying course could be laid out with some slight corrections in the present route. Egge had already announced on November 14, 1924, that such an overnight service would begin "in the spring of 1925."

A new and safer eastern terminal was constructed at

The cachet "OVERNIGHT AIR MAIL/FIRST TRIP-JULY 1, 1925/CONNECTING NEW YORK-CHICAGO appears on this cover to George Angers in Springfield, Massachusetts.

Hadley Field, five miles from New Brunswick, New Jersey. It was far enough away from New York City to avoid the pilot bugaboos of fog and smoke that plagued the current field, but it was close enough to be reached quickly by the fast mail trains running from New York to New Brunswick.

A field at Bellefonte, Pennsylvania, was equipped with

lights, beacons and radio towers to make it night operable as the first refueling stop. Several emergency landing fields were built along the night route. Each was at least 85 acres in area and run by a caretaker who tended the revolving searchlight and the field's boundary lights. All were connected by phone with the New York airmail radio station.

Though the transcontinental night flights over the Rockies had to soar to 14,000 feet or more, the much smaller Alleghenies presented a different problem. The Rockies offered an occasional flat plateau where a DH-4 could set down. The Allegheny country was steep, hilly and covered with trees. There were almost no emergency landing spots available. Some 150 beacons were spangled along the 770-mile airmail nighttime highway. In one dangerous 30-mile stretch between New Tripoli and Ringtown, Pennsylvania, five emergency landing fields were chiseled out of the timberland — each with a five-million-candlepower beacon.

Henderson's projected timing of "June 1 or sooner" never came off. In some rather high-flying prose, a Post Office press release of Sunday, June 28, reset the opening date as July 1, 1925. That press release charted the electrifying development of coast-to-coast communication beginning with the "crude stagecoach" that first offered 28-day overland service. This gave way to the pony express "whose mounted couriers traversed the Great American Desert in just nine days."

The Union Pacific was heralded next, and "faster and faster the mail trains sped until 87 hours from ocean to ocean was considered the ultimate in speed." The day-and-night transcontinental airmail "once more made the continent shrink, this time from 87 hours to 32 — a far cry from the stagecoach era of 28 days."

The ecstatic press release continued: "The hazardous

and tree-crowned Alleghenies have been studded with brilliant and powerful beacons to guide the air couriers of the night and warn them of dangerous peaks and crests as they wing their way through the darkness, while emergen-

Covers were carried on the first overnight mail service between New York and Chicago at the cost of 10¢ per ounce. This cover was carried on the Cleveland-New York leg.

cy landing fields have been literally carved out of the mountainsides to afford them refuge in time of mechanical trouble. Each day — Saturday and Sunday excepted — a plane will leave either city with the day's collection of airmail and arrive in the other with the dawn."

The rate for this new overnight service was set at 10¢ per ounce or fraction thereof. (The current daytime mail still went at 8¢ per ounce.) This change included transport by air, transport to and from the airmail route and anywhere beyond as far as 2¢ first-class postage would carry an ordinary letter. All stamps were good for airmail postage, though the Post Office advocated the use of the red, white and blue special airmail envelopes. Each letter also would have to be endorsed "Via Night Airmail."

In a *Postal Bulletin* of Wednesday, June 17, 1925, the

schedule was laid out. The eastbound mail left Chicago at 7:30 p.m. from the downtown post office and flew from Maywood Field at 8:30 p.m. Bryan, Ohio, was reached by 10:10 p.m. After refueling, the night airmail departed at 10:30 p.m. Central time, arriving at Cleveland by 1 a.m. Eastern time. Planes and pilots were changed here with take-off set for 1:20 a.m. Bellefonte, Pennsylvania, was to be made by 3:30 a.m., with a 3:50 a.m. departure carded after refueling.

The Chicago mail plane was scheduled to land at Hadley Field, New Brunswick, at 6 a.m., and by 7:30 a.m., the mail sacks were to arrive at the New York post office. Henderson assigned the very top pilots of the airmail service to the new night mail. There were 16 in all. Among them were such airmail aces as Dean Smith, J.D. Hill, Paul "Dog" Collins, Warren Williams, W.L. Smith and Shirley J. Short.

Chapter 25

First Night Flight

Wednesday night, July 1, 1925, was a beautiful evening in New York. At the new Hadley Field, some 15,000 people had gathered to watch the first Chicago-bound airmail plane take off on the regularly scheduled overnight flights between those two cities. Postmaster General Harry New was on hand, along with other postal and government officials. However, none of them had really anticipated the tremendous volume of mail posted for those first

This cover was flown on the first experimental test flight of the New York-Chicago overnight airmail service. It is postmarked Bryan, Ohio, June 16, 1925.

overnight junkets. Plans had been made for two aircraft if needed, and it was obvious from the volume of souvenir mail that both planes would fly.

The first plane, piloted by Dean C. Smith, took off ahead of time at 8:45 p.m. (To follow the elapsed time of the flights, it must be remembered that New York was operating on daylight-savings time in this particular period.) Dean Smith was a pilot who was used to flying in the dark. He had had plenty of experience on the Chicago-Cheyenne night-flying leg of the transcontinental Columbia route. That was one of the reasons he had been transferred to this new service. Smith's cargo consisted of about 90 pounds of mail.

Two hours after Smith left Hadley Field, a second plane took off. It was flown by J.D. Hill, one of the best and most experienced DeHavilland pilots in the corps. Hill's load was close to 300 pounds, and Postmaster New himself had helped load some of it into the DH-4. This heavy mail has one advantage for collectors: The New York-Chicago first-night covers are among the more numerous of the early airmail milestone flights.

But back to Smith in the earlier plane. He landed in Bellefonte, Pennsylvania, approximately two hours after leaving New York. Shortly after leaving Bellefonte at about 10 p.m. (Pennsylvania was not on daylight-savings time), Smith developed engine trouble that forced him down twice at Cuylerton, Pennsylvania, and Solon, Ohio. Pilot Art Smith was sent from Cleveland to nearby Solon to pick up the other Smith's mail. Art Smith flew nonstop into Chicago, touching down at Maywood Field at 8:20 a.m. Central time, July 2. Art Smith had taken all of Dean Smith's Chicago mail and left Dean the Cleveland cards and covers. After some more work on a pesky carburetor, Dean Smith carried only the Cleveland mail on into that city.

Meanwhile, in the second New York plane, J.D. Hill reached Cleveland at 2:15 a.m. Here he switched cargo and planes with pilot W.D. Williams, who delivered, at 6:19 that morning, a somewhat lighter load than Hill had

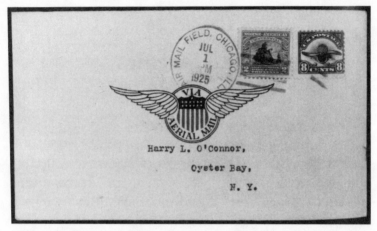

A July 1, 1925, first-flight cover of the Chicago-New York over-night airmail. The 2¢ stamp pays the rate for overnight service.

carried into Chicago. The second New York flight had beaten the first one by just two hours, but the elapsed time for D.C. and Art Smith was 13½ hours, while Hill and Williams had used but 9½ hours.

On the eastbound first nighter from Chicago, Shirley Short made it to Cleveland in under three hours. Paul "Dog" Collins took the 140 pounds of mail from Cleveland to New York and, arriving at 2 a.m., found himself at Hadley Field almost two hours ahead of schedule.

A second flight out of Chicago, flown by George Meyer and Charles Ames, made it into New York in just over seven hours. The new night airmail was pronounced an outstanding success. All covers flown on these flights, except for those posted at the airmail fields themselves, bear a cachet: "Air Mail — First Overnight Flight — New York to Chicago" (or "Chicago to New York").

Chapter 26

The Tragedies

The airmail's glory days from August 12, 1918, until August 31, 1927, comprise the period known to collectors and air historians as the "government era." It was during this time that the Post Office Department literally owned and operated the new airmail system. It hired, trained and paid the pilots. It recruited and directed all supporting ground personnel. It maintained the "Highway of Lights," as well as the newly developing radio network. It owned or leased the airfields from which its planes flew.

The commander-in-chief of the airmail was the postmaster general of the United States, and the airmail's executive officer was the second assistant postmaster general. The Post Office determined the rates, authorized the stamps and laid down the flying rules with some help and occasional hindrance from Congress. It was the time of total dominance by Washington over the airmail.

During those nine years, Uncle Sam — acting the role of benevolent despot — employed 2,700 people who were to pioneer some epoch accomplishments in air and postal transport. More than just pilots alone, this team included mechanics, clerks, field managers, radio operators, watchmen, laborers, truck drivers, beacon attendants and dozens of other workers who formed the payroll of the new airmail. These 2,700 people made the airmail work. They also made it expand and grow, first to Chicago then across the nation by day, then on to St. Louis, Milwaukee, St. Paul and Minneapolis, and finally to the supreme aerial goal — from coast to coast by day and night.

Many famous pilots came out of that government era and went on to carve out their own important careers in all phases of aviation. For now, I want to recall the airmail people who died during the government era. They, more than any of the others, dared the challenges of the new airmail and met its greatest adventures face to face. To a large degree, they are almost anonymous. Just once more let us see their names and record their passing.

The first pilot to perish was Carl B. Smith. He met death on December 16, 1918, while flying the airmail in a DeHavilland. The cause of the crash was not clear but ultimately was listed as "Smith's inexperience with this kind of plane." The year 1919 saw five airmail employees die — four pilots and a mechanic. The mechanic, August Thiele, was the first tragedy on January 8 of that year. He was struck by a propeller while starting an engine. Pilots Frank McCusker, Charles Lamborn, Lyman Doty and John Charlton also died in 1919. All but Doty were flying DH-4s. Doty was piloting a Curtiss ship. McCusker's plane caught fire in midair. He jumped some 200 feet to his death. Lamborn, flying at a low altitude, lost control of his plane in a fog and crashed. Doty smashed into a tree while attempting a forced landing. Charlton nosed over when trying a similar emergency landing.

In that year of 1919 the fledgling airpost flew a total of just 160,000 miles. With four pilots dying in service, that averages out to one airmail fatality every 40,000 miles — a high price to get a letter a few hours sooner.

In 1920, the airmail winged its way for 549,000 miles. Nine pilots died. Yet, the averages looked better — one death for each 61,000 miles flown. Six ground personnel also lost their lives that year, and if these were counted, the safety record was really the worst in airmail history to that date. The pilots who died were Clayton Stoner, Harry Sherlock, Richard Wright, Robert Gautier, Max Miller,

Pilot Walter H.S. Stevens was killed when his plane caught fire in a forced landing in Pemberville, Ohio. This cover, carried on the ill-fated New York-Chicago flight, bears the cachet, "Damaged Air-Mail Wreck/Near Toledo 0 9 14 20."

Walter Stevens, Frederick Robinson, Bryan McMullen and John Woodward. Ground personnel who were killed were mechanics N.C. Montis, Gustave Reierson and Russell Thomas; clerk Clarence Stapleton; helper Charles Nanista and Division Superintendent W.J. McCandless. A Jenny, seven DeHavillands, a Curtiss, a Martin and two Junkers-Larsons were involved in the air fatalities. One mechanic, Nanista, was killed in a prop accident.

Most of the deaths were caused by crashes during times of poor visibility. The Junkers ships, however, all caught fire in the air, and this flaming danger of the Junkers finally prompted the airmail service to abandon this plane entirely at a later date.

The death list for 1921 shows eight pilots and one mechanic. Miles flown that year by the service numbered 1,555,000. The total of nine deaths improved the safety record to one fatality for each 173,000 miles — if nine deaths can ever be regarded as an "improvement." The 1921 pilot fatalities included Kenneth Stewart, William Carroll, Hiram Rowe, William Lewis, Elmer Vanatta, James Christensen, Walter Bunting and Howard F. Smith. The mechanic was Robert Hill, who was riding

Pilot W.M. Bunting was killed when his plane crashed in Rock Springs, Wyoming, during the San Francisco-Chicago flight on May 5, 1921. In addition to the regular four-line cachet, this cover also bears a previously unknown cachet, "Damaged in wreck."

with Carroll. All of the planes involved were DeHavillands except for one Junkers-Larson, which killed three people in one crash. Most crashes this time were caused by engine problems or were ascribed to unknown reasons. Visibility and fog problems were almost gone now from the crash-cause listings — thanks to that confrontation by Leon Smith and Ham Lee, which led to the pilots being given full say so on whether they flew.

The year 1922 was a miracle one for the new airmail. Only one flying death was recorded all year, when pilot Walter Smith was killed as his plane went into a spin shortly after take-off.

The aerial grim reaper went back to work in 1923, however, when five pilots and a helper lost their lives. All six deaths occurred in the air. The pilots were Paul Oakes, Elmer Leonhardt, Harwell Thompson, Howard Brown and James Moore. Helper W.R. Acer was killed riding with Oakes. Nothing but DeHavillands crashed in that year of 1923, but by this time, there was hardly any other type of plane carrying the mail. Motor failures and the new specter of manufacturing defects were primarily responsible for the deaths — along with the freak accident caused by cows.

Pilot Harwell Thompson had made a safe emergency landing on September 7, 1923, in his mailplane No. 283. When attempting to take off, however, a few cattle suddenly veered directly into the path of his plane. Thompson swerved quickly, cartwheeled on his wings and was killed in the ground crash.

Three pilots died in 1924, and that year was happily the last one of multiple deaths in the government-operated airmail service. Leonard Hyde-Pearson and Clarence Gilbert both perished flying the mail. Gilbert's parachute failed to open as he jumped from his plane, while Hyde-Pearson's ship crashed and burned when he was forced down in a heavy snowstorm. The third pilot killed that year did not die on airmail duty. William Blanchfield crashed while scattering flowers over the grave of his mechanic friend, Samuel Gerran. This flight, though one of great compassion, represented an unauthorized use by Blanchfield of his DH No. 297. Mechanic Gerran's name does not appear on the roster of honor since he expired of an illness, not a flying accident.

In 1925, only Charles Ames crashed to his death flying over "Hell Stretch" in the Alleghenies. Pilot Art Smith was the lone fatality in 1926 when his Curtiss ship struck a tree and burned.

The last pilot to give his life in the government airmail service was John Milatzo, who crashed on April 22, 1927.

Snow and sleet had collected on his plane, forcing him into trying a landing in the dark on unknown terrain.

Over that nine-year span of glory, the honor roll of those who gave their lives for the new airmail includes 34 pilots, five mechanics, one clerk, two helpers and one division superintendent. One of those 34 pilots, Leonard Hyde-Pearson, must have had something of a premonition of his impending aerial death. He penned the following message to his fellow pilots with instructions that it not be opened until he had passed on. Written by one pilot to his own peers, it has to be one of the most fitting epitaphs of those who made the total sacrifice.

Hyde-Pearson's message reads like this: "To My Beloved Brother Pilots And Pals: I go west, but with a cheerful heart. I hope what small sacrifice I have made may be of some use to the cause. When we fly, we are fools, they say. When we are dead, we weren't half-bad fellows. But everyone in this wonderful aviation service is doing the world far more good than the public can appreciate. We risk our necks; we give our lives; we perfect a service for the benefit of the world at large. They, mind you, are the ones who call us fools. But stick to it boys. I'm still very much with you. See you all again."

Chapter 27

The Ghost Flight

In a personal sense, the early airmail history of the United States is a tale of death and sorrow. To build the aerial postal service — and the entire aviation system that was to follow — too many good men were called upon to face death and injury.

Of all these tragedies, perhaps the most publicized and heart-rending was the crash of Charles H. Ames on the final date of October 1, 1925. Ames began his aerial postman's duties on the Cleveland-New York leg in the early 1920s. When lighted airways came to that eastern airmail route in July of 1925, Charlie Ames was already a top-notch veteran aviator. For the new night airmail between New York and Chicago, none but elite pilots were chosen, and Ames was among the best.

Charlie's route in 1925 began at Hadley Field in New Brunswick, New Jersey. His first stop west was Bellefonte, Pennsylvania, for fuel and then onward to Cleveland. By mid-1925 this route was dotted with emergency landing fields about every 25 miles or so. At each field, a rotating beacon light guided the pilots by night and offered a sort of electrical security on the path over the Alleghenies — a geographical hazard that the pilots themselves referred to as "Hell Stretch."

The planes flown over this aviators' graveyard were DeHavilland DH-4s powered by the most powerful aircraft engine of its time, the Liberty 400. Charlie Ames' own DeHavilland was numbered DH-385. A rather crude group of instrument flying aids were just coming into the cockpits in this era, and when the weather got too soupy, a few pilots, including Ames, would resort to the new dials and gauges.

On the night of October 1, 1925, Ames lifted his DH-385 out of Hadley Field about 10 p.m. By the time he had

Charlie Ames' plane crash was one of the most publicized in airmail history.

been airborne for a few minutes, Bellefonte was already reporting some overcast skies at 1,500 feet. Other Pennsylvania stations were indicating visibilities as low as 10 miles. As Charlie Ames flew west the weather worsened quickly. One eastbound mail plane was held up at Cleveland and the airmail sent on via rail. Ames, however, was already well on his way.

When he reached "Hell Stretch," he was no doubt flying in total blackness with only his compass and clock to give him an idea of his actual location. His altimeter and the pressure on his barometer were the only instruments to judge his flying height.

The popular pilot never arrived at Bellefonte. After clocking him as overdue, that field telephoned Hadley and Cleveland, but each place reported no word from DH-385. All the pilots of that day were instructed to get to a phone and report immediately on any forced landings. No one had heard from Ames. All emergency landing fields and a few "farmer-spotters" were called. Thirty miles east of Bellefonte, the Woodward station reported having heard Charlie's plane on schedule apparently flying smoothly and at normal altitude. Another field related having seen Charlie's plane in flight. He was clearing the Allegheny ridges at a bare minimum height.

By the next morning Ames was officially listed as "missing." The *New York Times* and other papers gave the story front-page treatment. On October 3, the dense Pennsylvania fog began to lift, and every mail plane that could be spared began an aerial search from Clarion west to Bellefonte.

Carl Egge, the airmail superintendent, came to Clarion to command the search effort. Many pilot friends of Ames, including Harold "Slim" Lewis, flew to the area at their own request to join in. Ames' closest airmail buddy, Wesley Smith, came to help even though his wife was just about then giving birth to their first child. A Bellefonte mechanic, on his own weekend time and in his own car, started to comb the mountains east of Bellefonte. He was to pass within a few hundred yards of the downed plane without seeing it.

As the days went by without result, the quest for Charlie Ames became nationwide news. The mysterious suspense spawned the usual rumors and speculations — both printed and private. Had Ames really flown to Canada with the thousands in Wall Street securities that he was said to have carried in his mail sack? Had he absconded elsewhere after setting his plane down? Had a known infected knee and stiff leg caused him so much pain that he lost control and crashed?

The plane and Ames appeared to have vanished completely. By October 10, the substantial ground and air rescue effort had uncovered nothing — neither parachute nor smoke signal nor crash site.

The tale of Charlie Ames continued in the nation's newspapers, but it moved off the front pages as doubt

REWARD
$500

To the Person or Persons who FIND Pilot in Mail Plane Lost Thursday Night or Friday Morning.

NOTIFY Air Mail Field, Clarion, Pa.

This circular offered a $500 reward to anyone finding pilot Charlie Ames' mail plane.

grew that he would ever be found alive somewhere, someplace. The airmail service had offered a $500 reward to anyone who found the plane. This pecuniary incentive had increased the search parties somewhat but had been to no avail in finding what some reporters were now calling a "ghost flight."

East of Bellefonte is a spot called Nittany Mountain. It

even had a beacon light atop its highest point, but the caretaker of that station had reported seeing and hearing nothing of DH-385. Into that Nittany area on October 11 — 10 days after the last contact with Ames — came a ground search party containing a young boy named Johnny DeArmit. It was Johnny's 15th birthday, but he was spending it looking for the missing pilot.

It was Johnny who first saw the wreckage of DH-385 at Hecla Gap. Ames' body was still in the cockpit — his seat belt broken and his feet still wrapped around the control stick. That posture was a position pilots usually assumed when the flight was going well. They did it so they could rest their arms and relax. From this, investigators felt the crash was completely unexpected. In the black dark Charlie Ames had simply flown at full throttle into the Allegheny hillside. He had crashed into that mountain just 200 feet short of the beacon light in Hecla Park. The violent impact had pushed his head through the instrument panel and fractured his skull.

It was later determined that a mere two-tenths of a point error in the barometric reading could have meant the difference in clearing that ridge or slamming into it at full speed. Either Ames had misread it, or the instrument was not accurate enough. His friends and co-pilots, knowing Ames, tended to believe the latter.

The death of Charlie Ames was the 40th among the pioneer airmail pilots. From each fatality, hopefully, something was learned — be it about weather, plane, engine, controls, or, in Charlies case, instrumentation. Ames' death was, of course, a great loss to his family and many flying friends, but it is not unique from all the others save for one fact. When he flew into that Pennsylvania mountain, it began what was to become the longest search for a missing pilot in our early airmail history.

Chapter 28

The Kelly Bill

When the United States airmail celebrated its third birthday on May 15, 1921, it boasted more than 20 airfields, 75 planes, 55 pilots and 460 other employees, such as clerks, mechanics, radio operators and the like. Its operating routes were the New York-to-San Francisco Columbia cross-country main line, New York to Washington, St. Louis to Chicago, and Chicago to the twin cities of St. Paul and Minneapolis.

Airmail was still flying at the 2¢ rate, and in that first three-year period, the system had handled more than 80 million letters over more than 2.2 million flown air miles. Congress was not pleased with the airmail results and refused to appropriate sufficient funds to keep the total system going.

Just two weeks after the airmail's third birthday — on June 1, 1921 — the original New York-Philadelphia-Washington route was abandoned. Thirty days later, on July 1, the Chicago-St. Louis and Chicago-Twin Cities scheduled flights were scrubbed. Many government and postal officials had long felt that Uncle Sam should get out of the quasi-public business of owning and operating the airmail network.

From a political standpoint, the issue was somewhat of

a hot potato in those days of rugged individualism and the growth of private transit on all sides. Government ownership of the airmail was not popular with the voters of the United States, a fact politicians could easily sense. John Q. Public saw no reason why the government ran the airmail when it kept its nose out of the railroads, buses, truck lines and other forms of transportation.

This bugaboo of too much governmental control had much to do with the ultimate establishment of private airmail carriers. Among the elected officials who sensed

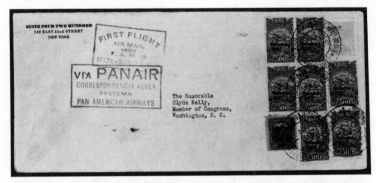

This first-flight cover from Brazil is addressed to Representative Clyde Kelly, who sponsored the famous Kelly Bill.

this was a Congressional representative from Pennsylvania named Clyde Kelly.

Chambers of commerce all over the United States had begun to bombard postal officials with pleas for airmail service to their own cities and towns. Among the loudest and best-organized of these groups was the Pittsburgh chamber. A delegation from Pittsburgh went to Second Assistant Postmaster General Paul Henderson with a strong and well-documented request for air service. Henderson told the delegation that the Post Office Department could do nothing until certain legislation, already pending in Congress, was acted upon. That legislation consisted of two bills in the House. The bills had been introduced by Clyde Kelly and Representative Fiorello LaGuardia of New York.

On December 5, 1923, Clyde Kelly had introduced H.R. 503 into the House of Representatives. That bill authorized the postmaster general to contract with any firm, individual or corporation for the transport of mail between such points as the postmaster general would designate. This first Kelly Bill set the rate of one mill per pound per mile as a fee to be paid the private carriers for such service and specified the airpost rate at 5¢ per ounce or fraction thereof "to be prepaid with distinctive stamps affixed."

LaGuardia's bill, dropped into the House hopper on February 13, 1924, gave the postmaster general similar powers in contracting with private carriers but also allowed the Post Office to keep operating the government service in any part of the United States that the postmaster general might deem necessary.

Postal officials were lukewarm toward both proposals. They did not like the fact that these pieces of legislation fixed a rate that was unsatisfactory at the time and, in effect, created a subsidy for private carriers by guaranteeing them a certain amount of tonnage payment on each flight. The postal official most involved with the eventual legislation that created Contract Airmail Service (CAM) was Harry New. New was a lame-duck senator from Indiana when Harding appointed him to the postmaster general's chair in 1923 to succeed Dr. Hubert Work of Colorado. Dr. Work — distressed and unhappy after operating under the duress of extreme budget-cutting measures during his short one-year term as postmaster general — had been named secretary of the interior, much to his relief.

Harry New was to serve under Harding and, for an additional six years, under Coolidge's administration. It was during the reign of New as postmaster general that CAM came alive and had its large initial growth. The displeasure of Harry New and other postal leaders with the first Kelly Bill caused that Pennsylvania congressman to come up with a revision. He put this before the House as H.R. 7064. This Kelly Bill gave the private carriers 80 percent of all the revenue derived from carrying airpost. The remaining 20 percent was to go to the government.

It was in this bill that the rates creating the 1926-27

The Kelly Bill created the zone rates that led to two of these three Contract Air Mail stamps.

CAM airmail stamps were espoused. Section nine of the bill said: "Special postage rates for this airmail service will be 10¢ for each route or fraction thereof on routes 1,000 miles or less; 15¢ on routes over 1,000 miles and less than 1,500 miles; and 20¢ on routes over 1,500, direct air mileage to control in each case."

Harry New did not like this bill either, but pressures were beginning to build that he could not stop. More cities were yelling for air service, and the heat was still being applied by the influential Pittsburgh Chamber of Commerce. In a parliamentary coup, the Kelly Bill was guided to Senate passage by Senator David Reed, also from Pennsylvania. Reed introduced the Kelly Bill, already passed by the House, into the Senate literally minutes

Postmaster General Harry S. New opens the first Contract Air Mail bids in September 1925.

before adjournment, and the anxious-to-leave senators okayed it unanimously. It was signed into law by President Coolidge on February 2, 1925 — the date when CAM officially could be said to have begun.

Postmaster Harry New did not give up, however, and in his annual report to the president on November 1, 1925, he asked that the bill be amended to allow the postmaster general to make contracts based at fixed rates per pound of mail. Kelly himself introduced this amendment to his Air Mail Act of 1925. The House passed it on May

29, 1925, with Senate approval coming just seven days later. Coolidge signed the amended bill on June 3, and Harry New had his victory over Clyde Kelly. The postmaster general now had authority to pay on a poundage basis that he would prescribe.

Airline operators were asked to bid for certain routes on July 15, 1925. These bids were opened on September 15. On November 7, 1925, the first five commercial airmail routes were awarded to these private companies: Boston to New York, Colonial Air Lines; Chicago to Dallas/Fort Worth, National Air Transport; Chicago to St. Louis, Robertson Air Craft Corporation; Elko to Pasco, Varney Airlines; Salt Lake City to Los Angeles, Western Air Express. Bids on three other routes were either unsatisfactory or still under consideration.

It is interesting to note that Ford Air Transport was not involved at all in these first five contract awards. The Ford contract was not signed until January 7, 1926; yet, Ford was the very first line to carry CAM mail. Within just 40 days after the contract was approved — on February 15, 1926 — Henry Ford's all-metal monoplanes would be winging the first CAM mail between Chicago, Detroit and Cleveland. The first five contractors were still trying to get going.

Chapter 29

CAM is Born

On March 3, 1919, a pilot named Edward Hubbard took off from Seattle, bound for Victoria, British Columbia. He was flying a C-700 open-cockpit biplane. His was a unique flight in United States airmail history for two reasons: First, Hubbard was carrying airmail for the Post Office Department in a private plane and getting paid for it. He was, therefore, the first forerunner of the manner in which all airmail is handled today — by private carrier. Ed Hubbard, in his C-700, was the first of the contract

This CAM No. 10 cover was carried on the first flight on the Miami-Fort Myers, Florida, route on April 1, 1926.

airmail (CAM) haulers. The second reason that flight was unique was that William E. Boeing, the builder of that C-700, was in the second cockpit.

Because the flight had to cross over open water, Boeing had equipped the plane with pontoons. Hubbard had been hired to fly mail into Victoria to catch the transpacific steamers that made Victoria their last port before heading for the Orient. William Boeing, still rather small as aircraft makers went even in those days, was interested in using these CAM flights as an outlet for some planes he had in mind. One such plane was the Boeing B-1 flying boat, a ship that Hubbard acquired and used to fly the mail over water until 1927. This was the aircraft that was largely responsible for establishing the name Boeing as a leader in airplane design and construction.

After Hubbard's successful venture, several other small contracts for feeder lines were awarded in various parts of the country. By 1926, a dozen such lines were in operation, and in the spring of that year, another event spurred the growth of contract airmail. Congress passed the Air Commerce Act, commonly referred to as the Kelly Bill. This act labeled it a duty of the secretary of commerce to foster the development of private, commercial aviation as quickly as possible. The ultimate objective was for private carriers to take over all routes, including the transcontinental schedule from New York to San Francisco.

Sometime in May 1926, the first deliveries were made on a new mail plane, the Douglas M-2. Fifty-one of these planes had been ordered. They had twice as much mail-carrying capacity as the DeHavillands, about 1,000 pounds. The M-2s were also twice as fast, and their greater operating range allowed the Post Office Department to close down refueling and maintainance stops at Bryan, Ohio; North Platte, Nebraska; Rock Springs, Wyoming; and Iowa City, Iowa.

The workhorse DeHavillands, which had been so vital to the attainment of coast-to-coast service, were used only on the San Francisco-to-Salt Lake City leg. From Salt Lake City all the way to New York, the new Douglas ships took over the mail.

On February 1, 1927, the Post Office Department took a giant step forward in simplifying the confusing zone rates. On that day, a new airmail postage rate of 10¢ per

This CAM cover was carried on the first flight of the Chicago-Dallas route. It is postmarked Kansas City, Missouri, May 12, 1926.

half ounce went into effect. For 10¢ the public could mail a letter anywhere in the United States without trying to figure out the old geographic or the mileage three-zone system. All you had to do was weigh it and pay by each half ounce. The first stamp issued for airmail after this new rate change was the 10¢ Lindbergh bearing an image of Lindy's Spirit of St. Louis and showing his flight route from New York to Paris. Lindbergh, incidentally, had been an airmail pilot on the Chicago-St. Louis feeder route before his historic flight.

The Kelly Bill had another important proviso: It allowed the postmaster general and the secretary of com-

On February 1, 1927, the airmail rate was set uniformly at 10¢ a half-ounce. This rate applied to government or contract airmail routes. This cover was carried on the first flight at the new rate.

merce, by joint order, to transfer ownership of all established airports and terminals to the municipalities in which they were located, subject to approval of the president. Thus, Congress had paved the way for the government to get out of the airmail service entirely — planes, airports and everything.

Post Office officials had made it plain from the start that they wanted to operate the airmail only as long as it took to demonstrate the workability and feasibility of airplanes carrying mail. Acting under the authority of the Kelly Bill, Postmaster General Harry New began to close down the government airmail service.

On November 15, 1926, independent airlines were asked to bid on the transcontinental route. The bids were to be entered in two sections: one for the New York-Chicago leg and another for the Chicago-San Francisco portion. Boeing Airplane Company and Edward Hubbard were successful in getting the San Francisco-Chicago route. (Boeing Airplane was later incorporated as Boeing Air Transport, Salt Lake City.) On June 30, Uncle Sam gave up his authority, and Boeing took over the schedule.

No acceptable bid was received on the Chicago-New York portion. In March 1927, this was re-advertised, and the bid of National Air Transport was accepted. The firm took over the route September 1, 1927; thus, on August 31 of that year, the government exited from the airmail service that it had begun on May 15, 1918.

Since these operators needed their own aircraft, some of the new Douglas planes were sold to them. But the balance of these new ships, along with the few flyable DeHavillands left, were transferred to other branches of government that needed them.

Many covers exist with the initial "C.A.M." stamped on the envelope, followed by a number. Before giving up the transcontinental route in 1927, the government had signed contracts with many carriers. By 1926, there were 12 of these. They are identified here by number, route, airline and date begun:

CAM 1 — New York-Boston, Colonial Air Lines (July 1, 1926).

CAM 2 — Chicago-St. Louis, Robertson Aircraft Corporation (April 15, 1926).

CAM 3 — Chicago-Dallas, National Air Transport (May 12, 1926).

CAM 4 — Los Angeles-Salt Lake City, Western Air Express (April 17, 1926).

CAM 5 — Elko, Nevada-Pasco, Washington, Varney Speed Lines (April 6, 1926).

CAM 6 — Detroit-Cleveland, Ford Air Transport (February 15, 1926).

CAM 7 — Detroit-Chicago, Ford Air Transport (February 1926).

CAM 8 — Los Angeles-Seattle, Pacific Air Transport (September 15, 1926).

CAM 9 — Chicago-St. Paul, Charles Dickinson (June 7, 1926).

CAM 10 — Atlanta-Jacksonville, Florida Airways (April 1, 1926).

CAM 11 — Cleveland-Pittsburgh, Clifford Ball (April 21, 1927).

CAM 12 — Pueblo, Colorado-Cheyenne, Western Air Express (May 31, 1926).

Colonial Air Lines got the first contract award, but the first actual carrier was Ford Air Transport. Owned by Henry Ford and operated for his auto company's needs as well as airmail, this Ford Air Transport venture begat the famous Ford Trimotor airplane.

Dickinson (CAM 9) lost four of his five planes in the first 90 days of operation. He was forced to quit, and Northwest Airways took over his route. Of all these carriers, Western Air Express was the first to get into large-scale (for those days) passenger service. It was an immediate success, and others followed.

Though airmail usage by the public was on the way up, most of these private carriers were averaging only 200 pounds per trip. To stimulate airmail volume, Congressman Kelly sponsored an amendment to his bill of 1925. Passed on May 17 and put into effect on August 1, 1928, it lowered the airmail rate to 5¢. This was the reason for the so-called Beacon stamp of 1928. This reduction was extremely costly to the Post Office, but since the carriers were paid on a pound-per-mile basis, the tremendous increase in airmail loads boosted profits substantially.

The critics went after the airmail again for subsidizing the private haulers. Postmaster New resisted the critics and told them he would hold to this 5¢ rate as an experiment for six months. It was a good "out" for New. By the time the six months were up, an election was under way.

In November 1928, Herbert Hoover was elected president, and along with him, into the postmaster general's chair, came a man named Walter Folger Brown. It was the beginning of a new era for the airmail. Brown was to make the rate decision and several others that changed forever the concept of contract airmail.

Chapter 30

The Boeing B-40

Out in the Olympic mountain area of the northwestern United States lived a wealthy young playboy-sportsman who was to bring to an end the age of the DeHavilland aircraft in American airmail annals. His name was William Edward Boeing. From his father he had inherited some large timber holdings in that Pacific Northwest area. He was immensely successful in the lumber business in his own right — but it bored him.

The dullness of the lumber game sent Bill Boeing into another pursuit: the designing and building of yachts. He bought a boat yard while still a young man and determined that he would build yachts, including one for himself. In 1914, a trip to Los Angeles changed his mind.

Boeing had seen an air meet and watched the great Glenn Curtiss in the sky. Though he was already a fisherman, hunter, sailor and yacht-builder, that sight made Boeing want something more. He wanted to fly. He went back to Los Angeles and enrolled in Glenn Martin's flying school. Martin had a small aircraft plant. After Boeing had soloed, he bought a plane from Martin and returned to Seattle.

When a friend cracked up the new plane, Boeing decided to build one of his own rather than wait six months for a replacement craft from the Martin plant. The boat yard was converted into an airplane plant. Boeing based his design on Martin's but made a few improvements and modifications of his own. From the time of its first flight, the first Boeing plane performed so well that the young

William Boeing (right) and pilot Eddie Hubbard return from a 1919 trial flight from Vancouver to Seattle. The plane is a Boeing C-700 seaplane. Boeing was to build his own planes that later flew many of the CAM and Foreign Air Mail routes.

playboy forgot all about yachts and turned all of his energies to the aircraft business.

When it seemed that war was imminent, Boeing hired designers, engineers and workmen, and forgot all other endeavors. He was going to make Boeing airplanes and sell them to the government. The unwillingness of Coffin, Deeds and others on the Aircraft Production Board to buy anything except foreign airframes for their Liberty engines caught Boeing by surprise. It left his new plant with little to do except to make a few Curtiss training planes under a special wartime contract. It was hardly enough work to stay in business. When the war ended, so did all production at the Boeing facility. Boeing was heartened when the new United States airmail system came into existence, but he soon realized that the new airmail was going to use up all the leftover planes from World War I.

Seeing little chance here, Bill Boeing decided he would go into the manufacturing of flying boats for commercial sale. His first attempt was the Boeing B-1. Pilots rated it as a superb aircraft, but no one bought any. It was this

This CAM 18 cover was carried on the first flight under contract from Chicago to San Francisco. It is postmarked Cheyenne, Wyoming, July 1, 1927. The cover is signed by Bill Schneider, Jr., who sent the cover, and pilot Frank R. Yager.

Boeing B-1 that chased the outbound ocean liners with last-minute overseas mail from Seattle to Vancouver.

When the government got out of the airmail service and began to take bids from contract airmail carriers, things looked a little brighter. When the Post Office Department abandoned the transcontinental Columbia route to private carriers, Bill Boeing saw his chance. That route was to be offered to private carriers in two sections

— New York to Chicago and Chicago to San Francisco.

Boeing started to design his first mail plane, realizing he might also have to get into the airline business as well. Everyone thought that the Chicago-San Francisco segment would go to Western Air Express, already a going concern. When the advertised bids for the route were opened in Washington, it was discovered that someone named Boeing had underbid Western by almost 50 percent. Boeing got the contract.

Such was the background behind the first really satisfactory airmail plane — the Boeing B-40. Bigger than the DeHavilland DH-4s, the B-40s also had a more powerful engine and could carry much more cargo. The B-40s made money for Bill Boeing from the start, in spite of the undercut bid. Much of the plane's success was due to a new rotary engine developed by Pratt & Whitney. It was called the "Wasp," and Boeing was able to get 25 of them for his new mail planes. The genius behind the Wasp engine was an engineer named Frederick Rentschler. He later became president of the Boeing Company.

Eventually, Boeing and Pratt & Whitney merged under

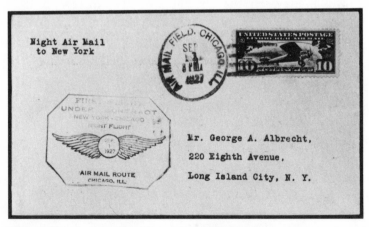

This CAM 17 cover was flown on the first night contract airmail flight from Chicago to New York on September 1, 1927.

a new corporate umbrella called the United Aircraft and Transportation Company. Picking up other aircraft suppliers, such as Hamilton Propeller and Sikorsky Aviation, the new United group suddenly jumped into national aviation prominence. The coast-to-coast airmail was now handled by Boeing's United concern in the west and by Clement Key's equally prominent National Air Transport in the east. These two giants were bound to clash, and they did. A series of political, economic and legal battles in the 1920s finally broke National Air Transport's exclusive hold on the Chicago-to-New York run and other eastern routes. United became the first airline in United States airmail history to fly mail from San Francisco all the way to New York City.

Other Boeing planes were to help expand the growing contract airmail service. These included the 40B4, the model 95 and the 221 Monomail, a single-winged plane that might have been the first of its type to haul mail since Ovington's Bleriot monoplane at Garden City. In more recent times, Boeing was the first to make a turbojet airliner, the famous 707.

Bill Boeing left the aircraft industry entirely in 1934. He returned only briefly for special service to his government during the World War II era. He died in 1956 at the age of 75, leaving behind two giants in the aviation field — the Boeing Company and United Airlines.

Chapter 31

The 'Flying Washboards'

The commercial or private carrier period started with contract airmail — more often and more simply referred to as "CAM." From May 15 to August 10, 1918, the United States Army Signal Corps pilots flew the mail under the supervision of the Post Office Department. On August 12, the government took over the airmail operation entirely, hiring the pilots, buying the planes and operating the airfields. Under the direction of the Post Office Department, the government also ran the ancillary services, such as the aviation radio system, pilot training, aircraft maintenance and many more.

In 1927, this direct governmental participation came to an end. The private carriers took over the flying of airpost and began the even larger potential business of carrying passengers. But that is jumping ahead of the story. The aircraft destined to fly the first CAM service were basically the creation of an American designer named William B. Stout (1880-1956). Though little known today, Stout was a pioneer in his field in the years before and after World War I.

From his childhood days when he first got a glimpse of Glenn Curtiss flying his immortal June Bug, Bill Stout was addicted to the science of aeronautics. He experimented with flying models long before the Wrights flew at Kitty Hawk, becoming an expert pilot in his own right in his adult years.

But the designing and building of aircraft were Stout's first love, and flying soon took a secondary role in his life. He founded and edited *Aerial Age,* but just writing about the fledgling aviation industry was not enough either.

William B. Stout autographed this first-day cover for the 6¢ airmail stamp honoring the Alexandria, Virginia, bicentennial.

Stout went to work for Packard, who, like many auto companies, was experimenting with aircraft and building the Liberty engine.

When war came, Stout was called to the Aircraft Production Board and assigned to McCook Field for developmental engineering work on the Jennies and DeHavillands. In those early years, most aeronautical engineers had one overriding goal: to get the largest amount of wing surface possible built into an airplane at the lowest total weight. The biplane seemed to satisfy this desire best; hence, the double-winged ships predominated.

In studying the DeHavilland DH-4, Bill Stout came to the conclusion that all of the extra bracing of wing wires and struts needed by that biplane created an unnecessary air drag that wasted most of the engine's power. That air-drag theory led him to design a monoplane that he described as "just a wing with control surfaces." The extra bracing was not needed since his exceptionally thick wing carried its own internal bracing.

Stout's bat-wing plane — a forerunner of the flying-wing concept of later times — was greeted with jeers and catcalls by other designers. It was nicknamed the "Cootie," an inglorious reference to the bug that infested many of the army camps and wartime trenches.

Not everyone laughed at Stout's concept, however. His mono-wing design was accepted by the National Advi-

This 1958 cover marked the re-enactment flight of the first contract airmail from Dearborn, Michigan, to Cleveland.

sory Committee for Aeronautics, and he was cited publicly for his work by the Aircraft Production Board. Even Orville Wright, after testing Stout's wing model in a wind tunnel, pronounced it as "probably the next great step forward in airplane design."

Bill Stout had long advocated the replacement of the familiar wooden propeller with one made of metal. He thought, why not make the entire plane of metal instead of wood and cloth fabric? In 1916, Stout built his first all-metal, thick-winged monoplane. The great Dutch designer, Anthony Fokker, also had been using the monoplane idea, but his first ships were fitted with wooden wings.

As an aside, it was in a Fokker wooden-winged craft that Knute Rockne crashed to his death in 1931. The air experts began to suspect dry rot in the wood, and a periodic inspection of all wooden planes was quickly ordered by the government. Rockne's death, coupled with the dificult inspection decree, doomed the Fokker planes from continued American use.

Meanwhile, in Detroit, Stout had made a post-war design of an all-metal monoplane for commercial transport service. Having no money of his own for manufacture, he wrote to 100 leading industrialists asking that they each invest $1,000 in his proposed airplane factory.

Stout had always been a gruff, outspoken, no-holds-barred sort of fellow, and his letters typified that demeanor. He frankly told the industrialists that "you will probably never see your $1,000 again." The letters brought in more than two dozen checks, each for the requested $1,000. Among the contributors was Edsel Ford, who also managed to get his rich and famous father, Henry Ford, to donate to Stout's cause.

The designer established a corporation, built an airplane plant and began to manufacture planes. In a factory near the Dearborn, Michigan, airfield — after some additional financial help from Henry Ford — Stout finally turned out five of his "flying washboards." They were all-metal, single-engined monoplanes powered by a Liberty motor. Henry Ford was so delighted with the ships that he bought all five and decided to start his own airline. Earlier, Ford had offered Glenn Curtiss his help in fighting what he termed "the Wrights stranglehold on the

American aviation business." He now offered that same help to Bill Stout. Soon Ford Transport Lines was a reality, flying daily schedules between Detroit and Cleveland and Detroit and Chicago. In 1925, those single-engined metal monoplanes made more than 1,000 trips between those destinations. In the first six months of that year, the planes carried nothing but freight, but beginning on July 1, they started hauling passengers as well. Most of the passengers were actually Ford executives flying on business trips in and out of Detroit.

It was also in July 1925 that Henry Ford bought William Stout's company — lock, stock and barrel. He paid the shareholders $2 for every $1 they had invested. He retained Stout on the Ford corporate staff, and the designer promptly began work on a new metal monoplane that was to be powered by three engines instead of one. That plane was to be Stout's undoing. He created the 3-AT, a

Bill Stout's ill-fated 3-AT Air Pullman that was destroyed by fire. It has many features that appeared in the famous Ford Trimotors.

ship that some air historians said may have had more things wrong with it than any other comtemporary flying machine. On the ground, it was ungainly, awkward, and ugly. In the air, it was an almost complete failure.

William Stout — one of the country's most heralded designers — had come up with a lemon. Henry Ford was unforgiving. Chagrined and disappointed, Ford saw to it that the plane and all blueprints and data pertaining to it were "accidentally" destroyed by fire. As far as Ford was concerned, the deficient 3-AT had never really existed.

Stout was taken off the assignment to produce a three-motored ship and, in Ford terminology, "sent to Nome, Alaska," in that company's executive hierarchy. With Stout out of the way, Ford turned the trimotor metal monoplane project over to a five-man committee consisting of John Lee, William Mayo, Otto Koppen, Harold Hicks and James McDonnell. The last-named member was later to found McDonnell Aircraft. These five men, with Stout on the sidelines, were to develop the fabulous Ford "Tin Goose." It is better known as the Ford Tri-motor, one of the great aircraft in aviaton history and one that was to play a vital role in the CAM system.

Chapter 32

Ford Air Transport

A quick epitaph on Henry Ford might read something like this: Henry Ford (1864-1947) — Inventor of the mass production assembly line — Maker of America's first low-priced auto, the "Model T" — Originator of a unique auto marketing maxim that said, "Give 'em any color they want as long as it's black."

It is one of Mr. Ford's lesser accomplishments, however, that intrigues the airmail collector and historian. In 1925 Ford began his own airline called Ford Air Transport. To fly it, he developed and financed the first all-metal American monoplane. The first planes used on the route were Ford single-engined ships. The famed Trimotor "Tin Goose" did not make its appearance until the line had already been in operation flying cargo and passengers for about a year.

On January 7, 1926, Postmaster General Harry New signed a contract with Ford Air Transport to carry mail between Detroit and Cleveland and also between Detroit and Chicago. Though Ford was by no means the first to obtain a government airmail contract under the revised Kelly Bill, he was the first of all the early CAM operators to actually get the mail into the air.

Ford Air Transport lines had its hangars at the Dearborn, Michigan, airport. On the first day of CAM in the United States, February 15, 1926, a rather sizable parade of postal, Ford and local dignitaries marched from Detroit to the Dearborn field for the inaugural CAM flight. Approximately 72 pounds of mail was placed into a "Tin Goose" that was to be piloted by Larry Fritz. At 10:40 a.m., pilot Fritz took off from the Dearborn facility. He landed at Cleveland's Municipal Airport one hour and 17

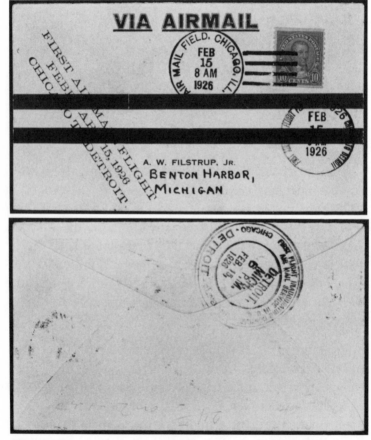

This CAM 7 cover carries the cachet "FIRST AIR MAIL FLIGHT/FEBRUARY 15, 1926/CHICAGO TO DETROIT."

minutes later after a routine, uneventful journey. CAM was not only off and running, its first trip had been completed 20 minutes ahead of schedule.

Fritz also flew the westbound CAM mail from Cleveland back to Detroit, leaving Cleveland at 2:30 p.m. that same afternoon and arriving back in Dearborn at 4:15 p.m. On this return trip he carried just 36 pounds of the

This first CAM flight cover from Detroit to Cleveland bears two of the large, cartwheel-style cachets that were to identify many first CAM flights until mid-1927.

new CAM airpost. Also on February 15, 1926, Ford Air Transport flew CAM mail over the second leg of its government contract: Detroit to Chicago. This route was tagged CAM 7.

The familiar cartwheel-style cachet marking was applied to almost all of the first flights from the inception of CAM up until mid-1927. This distinctive large cachet makes early CAM covers very easy to spot. It also makes them desirable material for other cover collectors searching for unusual postmarks. Airmail collectors probably will find the supply of CAM covers less abundant in the years ahead as the non-airmail cover collecting fraternity enters into competition for them.

As CAM service spread rapidly to other cities in the United States, the only eventual remaining government-operated route was the Columbia transcontinental service from New York to San Francisco. On June 30, 1927, the last government planes flew the Columbia. July 1 of that year saw National Air Transport and Bill Boeing's new company complete the coast-to-coast link of private carrier airmail. On that date, for all practical purposes, Uncle Sam stepped out of the airmail business. The era of government-operated flights was over.

Chapter 33

The Dictator

When Walter Folger Brown became postmaster general under Hoover, the airmail network was composed of relatively small airlines flying a multitude of short schedules. When Brown left office four years later, the great airlines as we know them today had started to emerge. Those four years were probably the stormiest, most controversial and, in the opinion of some, the most productive ever turned in by a postmaster general of the United States.

Just who was Walter Folger Brown, and how did he accomplish that remarkable task in just about 48 months? Brown was a lawyer in Toledo, Ohio, and something of a local and national power in Republican politics. He was influential in helping Herbert Hoover secure the nomination for president in 1928. For his work, Brown was appointed postmaster general.

When Brown became postmaster general, he insisted on a huge limousine — far grander than some other cabinet members had. When friends chided him about this flamboyance, his reply was that he had a top-hat job and he was going to have a car that could comfortably accommodate a top hat. Anyone who didn't like it knew what he could do.

Brown took his political appointment seriously, however, and began a study of both the aviation industry and the airmail service. He came to the conclusion that mail revenues for the airlines should be a sideline, much as they were for the railroads. Passengers should be the airlines' number one revenue maker. If this could be done,

Postmaster General Walter Folger Brown, a stormy, controversial and productive figure.

the charges to the Post Office Department for carrying mail would be greatly reduced.

The only airlines that could prove this theorem, Brown concluded, were the larger, well-financed lines that had adequate equipment, personnel and resources. His ultimate goal was a transcontinental network of a few large lines, strongly financed and competing with each other.

After two years of thoroughly learning the airmail system, Brown came out into the open when, in February 1930, he recommended passage of the McNary-Watres Act — another amendment to the original Kelly Bill. It was obvious that Brown saw himself as the only man who could lead the airlines in the way they should go. That act, passed by Congress on April 30, 1930, had four major provisions:

1. It changed the old pound-per-mile rate into a standard rate of $1.25 per mile for cargo space — whether that space was full or empty of airmail.

2. It gave Brown the power to extend or consolidate contract airmail routes "where the public interest was promoted." The evalutation of this "public interest" was left up to Walter Brown.

3. No contracts could be awarded to an airline that had not satisfactorily completed a daily flight schedule over routes at least 250 miles long for a minimum of six months.

4. Any airline with two years of successful and safe operation could exchange its contract for a certificate good for 10 years, unless otherwise revoked for good and sufficient reason by Walter Brown.

Suddenly, Brown had been given a lot of power — far too much in the opinion of many airline operators and others. As Brown himself stated, the bill rather excluded the small airline and favored the larger ones. He is quoted as explaining this as follows: "We are not buying peanuts and pencils . . . we are buying an extremely specialized and hazardous service . . . there is no sense in doling out government money to every little fellow flying around the map and not going to amount to anything . . ."

Ben Lipsner said that Brown felt that if Uncle Sam was going to encourage airlines to carry passengers, the government became "responsible in a way" for the safety of those passengers. Thus, Brown believed the power to re-voke certificates was necessary for the public's protection.

The old concept of the lowest bidder getting the con-tract was not, by Brown's definition, condusive to the development of larger, better planes and passenger safety. To avoid competitive bidding, Brown used his power to extend present airmail routes of the larger airlines compa-nies. He also held that transcontinental routes would not be successful unless they were operated by one airline under one management. Accordingly, on August 25, 1930, bids were asked on two long transcontinental routes. American Airways won the southern route, al-though it bid it at the maximum rate. For the northern route, Brown practically forced the merger of Western Air Express and Transcontinental Air Transport, thus creat-ing the company we know now as TWA.

By the spring of 1931, Brown's somewhat dictatorial methods had created an airmail network that looked like this: TWA and American Airways handled all north-cen-tral and southern routes; United flew from Chicago to Seattle, Chicago to Dallas, and another route north and south along the Pacific Coast; Eastern Air Transport was all alone up and down the East Coast.

Brown often forced airlines to take on additional routes they really didn't want — and added 9,000 miles of such schedules. In almost all of these route extensions, a small, independent airline was forced out of business. It was a ruthless, high-handed and effective way of getting what Brown wanted.

When Franklin Roosevelt won the election in 1932, Brown was out, and a new postmaster general, James A. Farley, took over. Brown left behind an airmail system of 34 routes flying 27,000 miles of airway. He had reduced the cost of airmail to the government from $1.10 per mile in 1929 to 54¢ per mile when he departed. As Lipsner said, it was an impressive record "if you could ignore the dead bodies at the side of the road . . ."

When the new administration took office, it saw, in the record of Walter Brown, a chance to attack its opponents and make some solid political points. Under Senator Hugo Black, a special Senate investigating committee — originally formed to look into overseas airmail — turned its attention to Walter Brown. Brown's dictatorial methods had made him an ideal target for investigation. He was charged with — among other things — collusion with the major carriers for personal gain, elimination of competitive bidding practices, and making illegal prearranged contracts with a few favored airlines. The results of the Black Committee led to a presidential order that stopped the development of airmail and airmail carriers cold, and delivered a blow to the airlines from which they would be a long time recovering.

Chapter 34

The Interlude

Senator Hugo Black's committee, which began the investigation of ex-postmaster General Walter Brown, had one thing in common with 1973's Watergate Senate Committee: It had no power to find anyone guilty or not guilty. Like Senator Ervin's group, Black's committee could only try to determine the facts as best it could to see if recommendations for further action were necessary.

The Black Committee hearings began in September 1933 while Brown was still in the postmaster general's chair. When they ended, the evidence of collusion, favoritism and other charges seemed strong and substantial enough for Roosevelt and Farley.

One of these charges was that a so-called "spoils conference" took place in May and June 1930. At this meeting, Brown and the major airlines supposedly had split up all the airway routes in the United States among those attending. On February 9, 1934, President Roosevelt, basing his decision on what he saw as fact, suddenly canceled every airlines contract in existence. The commanding general of the Air Corps, General B.D. Foulois, was summoned to the Oval Office and asked if the Army could once more fly the mail. After all, it had done so once, back in 1918, and should be able to do it again.

As later events proved, the Air Corps was not exactly in a state of readiness. It had suffered for some years from lack of funds, lack of new equipment and a resultant lowering of morale. Roosevelt was adamant that the Air Corps could do the the job. Perhaps in the hope of better

Front of a leaflet denouncing Roosevelt's cancellation of air-mail contracts in February 1934. Twelve Army pilots subsequently lost their lives flying the mail.

treatment in the years ahead, General Foulois agreed that the Air Corps was ready and capable.

The commercial airlines were to make their last airmail flight on Feburary 19. The cancellation was a severe blow. In the few preceding years, the carriers had made an effort to become financially independent of airmail revenues by seeking passenger business. They had made some progress, and passenger income was mounting each year. But they were not ready to operate with passengers only. They needed the mail revenue, and badly.

Just at this time a new airplane — the Douglas DC-2 —

appeared on the scene, and many lines had contracted for several of these new ships. Ironically, the first day before the airmail was taken away from commercial airlines, a DC-2 had flown from Los Angeles to Newark with 14 passengers plus mail to set a new coast-to-coast record of

The cachet on this February 20, 1934, cover reads, "Inaugurating/ARMY AIR MAIL/SERVICE/FROM/'The Busiest Airport/in the World'/NEWARK, N.J."

13 hours plus. That flight carried the last mail to be handled by the commercial carriers.

The Army's new assignment got off to a tragic start. Three days before the Army mail takeover, four Army pilots en route to their new mail flight assignments crashed. Three of the four were killed; the fourth was critically injured. In the first few days after February 19, five more pilots died, and six more were injured. Eight planes were lost in these crashes. The property loss to the taxpayers was some $300,000.

Although Farley had cut the 27,000-mile commercial routes to just 11,000 miles for the Army, things did not improve. On February 22, two more pilots came down, and the following day another lost his life. The costly destruction of men and machines went on throughout February and into March.

In early March, Roosevelt ordered a severe cutback in airmail service and sent a stinging reprimand to the secretary of war, telling him to put an end to the terrible crashes. At this point, airmail took a 10-year backward step. It resorted to daylight-only flying, and then only in good weather conditions. The very best Army pilots were assigned to mail duty.

None of these moves seemed to help. On March 9, four more pilots died. Roosevelt had to act once more. This time, on March 10, he proclaimed that the airmail would

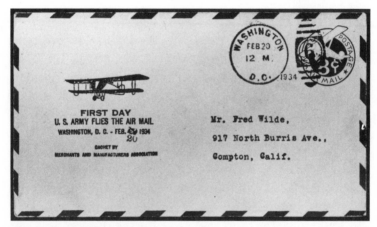

This cover marked the first day of the Army emergency flights of 1934. It is postmarked Washington, D.C., February 20, 1934.

be returned to the private carriers just as soon as possible. He also offered an eight-day shutdown of all airmail service to give the Army some time to regroup and rework its equipment.

This didn't help either. On March 31, the twelfth pilot went to his death. Postmaster General Farley called the airline operators to a special meeting on April 20. Here bids were taken for airmail routes but only under a special Farley proviso: No airline could win a contract if it or its personnel had been in attendance at the famous spoils conference and done business with Walter Brown.

To meet this regulation — or more factually stated — to get around it, the carriers had reorganized. Executives who had dealt with Brown were replaced. American Airways changed its name to American Airlines, Transcontinental and Western added "Inc.," and became TWA Incorporated. Eastern Air Transport turned into Eastern Airlines, and somewhere along the way, Varney Speed Lines had become Continental. Many of the famous names that are so familiar to us today were born of Farley's edict.

Not only had the Army sustained heavy losses of life and equipment, its cost of flying the mail — according to some later accounting analyses — was about $2.20 per mile compared to the 54¢ per mile cost of private transport. It was Lipsner's guess that it took the airlines until 1939 to recover from what he called the "body blow of contract cancellations."

Whether that is true, the last irony of the horrible Army experiment came on July 14, 1941. A United States court rendered the verdict that the charges brought against Walter Brown were untrue. There had been no collusion, no fraud and, thus, no real need for the disastrous Army interlude in United States airmail history.

Conclusion

For me, the beginning of CAM and the ending of the government flights really writes "finis" to the most vital and dynamic period of United States airmail history. It was during the pioneer government-operated era that the airmail was born, flew westward out of its New York-Philadelphia-Washington cocoon, conquered the treacherous Alleghenies and Rocky Mountains, spanned the nation from coast to coast and embarked on the great adventure of flying in the dark in all kinds of weather. It was the era of the inadequate Jennies and the workhorse DeHavillands. It was the age of the giants in our airmail development — Max Miller, Ed Gardner, Reuben Fleet, Ham Lee, Jack Knight, Ben Lipsner, Otto Praeger and many, many more.

It was the epoch stage of the open biplanes and unbelievably courageous men, flying more by raw instinct than precision and often freezing half to death in their rabbit-fur suits stuffed with old newspapers. It was an exciting, daredevil, romantic, foolhardy, undisciplined, glorious sort of time. With the coming of CAM, it was gone forever. We shall not see its like again.

Photo Credits

Dan Barber collection: pages 53, 55, 122, 142, 147, 150, 156, 157, 160, 161, 166, 176

Roderick B. Dyke collection: pages 132, 133

A.D. Jones collection: pages 18, 34, 51, 59, 68, 73, 77, 78, 79, 97, 100, 123, 125, 149, 177

National Philatelic Collection, Smithsonian Institution: pages 6, 11, 13, 33, 57, 60, 61, 69, 84, 91, 98, 102, 107, 112, 155

Patrick A. Walters collection: pages 38, 42, 43, 65, 72, 81, 82, 95, 99, 102, 108, 118, 119, 120, 127

Index

181

D

E

F

G

H

J

K

L

M

V

W

Y

The Author

Fred Boughner was born in Cadillac, Michigan, in 1923. He graduated from the University of Toledo, where he majored in economics and minored in journalism, doing part-time work for the *Toledo Blade*. For 37 years, Boughner worked as a packaging salesman for Owens-Illinois, Inc., in Oklahoma City and Dallas, and district sales manager in Kansas City and Houston.

A stamp collector for many years, Boughner began specializing in the airmail field in the mid-1960s. Fascinated by the tales about early pilots and their flights, he began collecting stories behind airmail stamps and covers.

From 1973-77, Boughner authored the weekly "Airmail Antics" column in *Linn's Stamp News*. After a total of 204 articles, he began "Official Antics" as a five-month change of pace. This series concentrated on carrier stamps and free-franked mail.

"Airmail Antics" again began reappearing in 1979.

Following retirement from Owens-Illinois in 1980, Boughner joined *Linn's Stamp News* as features editor.

In May 1981, Amos Press, the parent firm of *Linn's*, launched *Stamp World* magazine and named Boughner associate editor. By the end of that year he had been promoted to editor.

Following the demise of *Stamp World*, Boughner assisted Amos Press in the establishment of *Software Supermarket* magazine and in the transition of Scott Publications from New York to Sidney, Ohio. He edited the *Scott Monthly Journal* until a permanent editor could be found.

In 1984, Boughner was named manager of ancillary products for *Linn's* and began authoring the annual series of *Linn's U.S. Stamp Yearbooks*. After completing the 1987 *Yearbook*, the fifth in the series, he retired from Amos Press in early 1988.

Boughner resides in Sidney, Ohio, with his wife, Elaine.